Open Up Heart and Sunshine In.

CW00859903

Tony Kearney

ISBN 978-1-326-71996-8
Copyright © Tony Kearney 2016

Contents

A man finds himself, to his great astonishment, suddenly existing, after thousands of years of non-existence; he lives for a little while; and then, again, comes an equally long period when he must exist no more. The heart rebels against this, and feels that it cannot be true.

The only business of the head in the world is to bow a ceaseless obeisance to the heart.

I love those who can smile in trouble, who can gather strength from distress, and grow brave by reflection. 'Tis the business of little minds to shrink, but they whose heart is firm, and whose conscience approves their conduct, will pursue their principles unto death.

Love is space and time measured by the heart.

The moment you have in your heart this extraordinary thing called love and feel the depth, the delight, the ecstasy of it, you will discover that for you the world is transformed.

Where the Mind is biggest, the Heart, the Senses, Magnanimity, Charity, Tolerance, Kindliness, and the rest of them scarcely have room to breathe.

Educating the mind without educating the heart is no education at all.

There never was any heart truly great and generous that was not also tender and compassionate.

The things that we love in our heart tell us what we are.

Your vision will become clear only when you can look into your own heart. Who looks outside, dreams; who looks inside, awakes.

Enough of science and of art; Close up these barren leaves; Come forth, and bring with you a heart that watches and receives.

Every heart sings a song, incomplete, until another heart whispers back. Those who wish to sing always find a song. At the touch of a lover, everyone becomes a poet.

And now here is my secret, a very simple secret; it is only with the heart that one can see rightly, what is essential is invisible to the eye.

While you are proclaiming peace with your lips, be careful to have it even more fully in your heart.

The Divine Spirit does not reside in any except the joyful heart.

An artist needn't be a clergyman or a churchwarden, but he certainly must have a warm heart for his fellow men.

There is no charm equal to tenderness of the heart.

'Tis the business of little minds to shrink; but he whose heart is firm, and whose conscience approves his conduct, will pursue his principles unto death.

The Heart is Forever Inexperienced.

I was never really insane except upon occasions when my heart was touched. Let my heart be still a moment and this mystery explore.

Where the mind is biggest, the heart, the senses, magnanimity, charity, tolerance, kindliness, and the rest of them scarcely have room to breathe.

The human heart has hidden treasures. In secret kept, in silence sealed. The thoughts, the hopes, the dreams, the pleasures, whose charms were broken if revealed.

When we die we live on in the hearts of others.

I prosper that it is better to have a heart without words than words without a heart.

A loving heart is the beginning of all knowledge.

My heart has followed all my days, something 1 cannot name.

Afterword.

Introduction

Not so long ago my brother in New Zealand discovered a long lost audio tape made by my family (on one of those old reel to reel tape recorders) way back in the annals of time when the world was being swept along by the early throes of Beatlemania and I was a mere eight years old. We had made this tape for the purpose of sending it to a relative in Ireland (where coincidentally enough I now live). Although whether or not it was ever actually sent to her I do not know.

My brother managed, with the marvels of modern technology, to transfer this old reel to reel tape recoding on to a digital format and sent me a copy to listen to. We all knew about this tape but thought it had been lost forever and so it was quite a thing to hear it again with the long lost voices of my Grandmother, my parents, my siblings and indeed myself when I used to be me!

I remember being a big fan of the Beatles at the time, as we all were, but on the tape there is a brief snippet of me singing a cover version of the Manfred Mann hit Do Wah Diddy Diddy. Perhaps the title of the song was a prophetic sign of things to come in my life?

Who knows? But I do remember when we made the tape in 1964, and I am sure my Grandmother had a tipple in her when it was made as she is very funny talking on the tape and about this new fangled gadget called a tape recorder which she was very suspicious of!

It was also very sweet to hear my parents asking me things about school hoping that I might be give sensible answers to their questions to impress the relatives from so far away but little did they know at the time that the child is the father of the man!

For when they ask me at one point the classic question of – "What do I want to be when I grow up?" - I respond by saying that I won't know until I grow up! At this point I think they kind of resign themselves to the fact that maybe I might be the black sheep of the family and move on to question another sibling in the hope of getting some sense out of them instead.

Listening to the tape brought back so many memories of growing up in New Zealand during the 1960's. Of course one tends to look through rose tinted glasses, but in many ways I didn't have to look through such glasses because it was a happy time growing up in a clean, safe, happy and healthy environment. We didn't know that it was like that because we were the goldfish in that particular goldfish bowl and it was all we knew. But looking back with what I know now I realise just how lucky I was.

One of the memories I have of that time was of my mother's older sister Auntie Marie and her husband Uncle Vic. They were childless themselves and so they loved having their nieces and nephews (of which there were many) over to stay or visit, and whilst we were there they kept us totally entertained with Uncle Vic and his bag of tricks and magic and Auntie Marie with her love of music and the Pianola in the front room, which if we were really good we might get a chance to play.

It was amazing sitting on the piano stool and stretch your too short legs down to the pedals of the Pianola and push them up and down to try and play all these amazing tunes that she had.

Plus, she had her old vinyl records and she would play us some of the classic tunes she loved and teach us some of the songs too.

One of the songs she loved was Rosemary Clooney (herself the auntie of the now famous George Clooney) and her sister Gail singing the song:

Open Up You Heart and Let the Sunshine In.

We loved it!

Looking back with those older eyes again, one can see things about the song that one couldn't see with the eyes of innocence, such as the Christian subtext, the politically incorrect messages about the nasty "devil" and so on, but sometimes the eyes of innocence are to be preferred to those of so called experience.

For what carried us along in our sing song was the chorus line of:

Smilers never lose,
And frowners never win.
So open up your heart and let the sunshine in.

And it did!
Because we were all happy singing along in Auntie Marie's wonderful children's chorus. Because it didn't really matter **what** we were singing for something inside was singing whilst we were singing.

Now many years later in thinking about writing this book with a possible message for us all in these times I cast my mind back to those days and that song and the joy I felt being with someone who was able to transfer and share the simple pleasures of life and love.

Cynicism and conspiracy theories were absent from those experiences. It was enough to be with someone who loved you and in something together. There was nothing missing because there was nothing else we needed.

Our hearts were open and things were exactly where they needed to be.

Our modern world is a lot faster and a lot more troubled than that world of 50 plus years ago. No it wasn't perfect then and nor is it now.

But there is something to be said for opening up one's heart and letting the sunshine in. Because the sunshine brings the two most important ingredients to sustain all life here on Earth: – light and warmth. Far better to let those things in than problems, blame, bitterness and regret.

So I have chosen the title of that song as the title for this book. I have however added a little bit to the title as well, for I think that it is only half the equation to the let the sunshine in. It is equally upon us to let a little bit of that natural sunlight we all carry out also.

Imagine how bright the world would be if everyone let some sunshine out at the same time.

And imagine how much more sunlight might flood in from the Sun itself if we did so.

Fiat Lux – let there be light.

After all, that is what we are all made of and that means we must all be related.

Which might be why Jesus Christ would say:

"Do unto others as you would have them do unto you."

For, they **are** you!

It just doesn't seem like they are until you get to know them better.

And what is the way to get to know them better?

Well, open up your heart and let the sunshine in of course! ☺

The Heart of the Matter can only be seen from Afar.
The Afar of the Matter can only be seen from the Heart.

Most people have heard the first part of the title of this chapter at some point in their lives. It is taken to mean that a person can't see the truth of what something is, or what the truth of any given situation is if one is too close to it. It's a bit like the saying that one cannot see the wood for the trees.

Another way of looking at this is that it is only with context and perspective and what might be termed the bigger picture that the true reality can be properly discerned.

For without the bigger picture view one can tend to think that one's own version of the truth is in fact the truth, the whole truth and nothing but the truth. But rarely is this the case. For if a person is personally involved and too close to what is going on, then it is very hard to have an objective view of what is actually happening in any given situation. And if a person's view isn't objective then it must be subjective.

This is what the empirical study of science tries to achieve - a rational and objective understanding of life, the Universe and everything in it and how it works. Within which the experimental method tries to eliminate bias and subjectivity. However, the problem here is that it is always a scientist that designs the experiment and also is the one who measures and interprets the results and findings.

This difficulty of not being able to see what the truth of something is applies equally to the scientific method as it does to a person being too closely connected to the events that they are looking at. For if a person looks at a rabbit then one has a reasonably good idea of what it is. (Although if one has never seen a rabbit before how does one actually know what it is?)

However, if one then takes one strand of hair from the rabbit can one say that one is still looking at a rabbit? Or indeed its nose, foot, heart, lungs or eyes?

It seems that the sum is greater than that of the individual parts.

But then if one takes that hair from the rabbit's fur and paces that hair under the microscope and looks at it then one can begin to see the finer and finer particles that go to make up that individual hair. But is one still looking at a rabbit?

Then if one replaces the ordinary microscope with an electron one then it is possible to look into ever and ever smaller spaces of what goes to make up the individual hair itself. This extends down to being able to look into the constituent parts of not only each and every cell that goes to make up the hair of the rabbit but to peer into the individual atoms themselves and the small Universe that exits within every atom. And with ever improving technology it is possible to look into the smaller and smaller worlds of the atom until .... matter actually disappears! Because at some point the very thing that one is looking at changes from being something to being ..... nothing!

But not nothing in the normal sense of how that word is used, but nothing in the sense of - no thing.

So instead of being matter, which appears to our eyes as being tangible and real, the thing being looked at ceases to be physical any more and reverts back to the state it was in before it became matter - energy.

For everything in the physical world begins and ends its "life" as energy, for matter is really nothing more than condensed energy that began its life's journey into becoming matter as light in some far off star in some far off galaxy somewhere in the Universe millions of light years from here and yet from the same place before time and space began.

Whatever happened to our poor wee bunny rabbit?

It has disappeared in to the ether (from where it came in the first place) because it has been looked at too closely! Yet it itself is still there and alive and well and completely unaware that it has "disappeared" because it has been looked at too closely. Best not to tell it that it doesn't exist in case it comes as something of a nasty shock.

In fact, this has been one of the consuming passions of science in recent decades - the search for what is called the Higgs Boson or as it is sometimes known (to the chagrin of many scientists) the God Particle. This is the search for how and why "stuff" exists or why matter exists, and how and why it condenses. To find this out one apparently needs a Large Hadron Collider that is capable of blowing up the smallest known particles of matter so that one can then find out how and how it came to be matter in the first place!

This could be a most excellent example of what is being spoken about in the first part of this chapter which is that the heart of the matter can only be seen from afar.

For no matter how many rabbit cells one explodes in a collider, and no matter how many individual cells of the rabbit one assembles in a giant petri dish neither, will actually reveal what a rabbit is and what it does and more importantly of all where it ultimately comes from. And regardless of how many scientists from all around the world one gathers in to a laboratory, none of them can assemble an apparently random group of protons, neutrons and electrons and ultimately even cells in to a rabbit's hair yet alone a rabbit.

Given that there are upwards of a trillion cells that go to make up a rabbit, and if one was to place the poor rabbit in to a centrifuge (or a large Hadron Collider if you have a spare one in the back garden) and dice up the creature in to a blobby mass on a plate, no one could or would say it is or was a rabbit. But if we spare the rabbit from this nasty collider and put it on the ground to run and jump around as rabbits do, then everyone would be able to easily identify it as being a rabbit. It is simple to distinguish from a cat, even though they probably have a similar number of cells and therefore a similar number of atoms and protons, neutrons and electrons.

Yet if one was faced with a large bowl of random cat cells on one side and another bowl of random rabbit cells on the other it would be impossible to tell without knowing beforehand which bowl was the cat and which was the rabbit. And neither would the cat or the rabbit know what they were either!

So we can't find out what something is by analysing or dissecting it or invading its space or by changing its coherence into a state of chaos or apparent randomness.

What gives a thing its sense of coherence?
What is the blueprint that gives something a template

around which it can and does form up and turn into a living shape that we recognise and can identify?

Perhaps this is where Einstein can help with his theory of relativity?

For what something is unto itself is relative to what everything else is relative to the thing that we are trying to find out what it is by relating it to everything else! So a thing is everything it is not excepting of course what it is, but what it is can only be understood by understanding everything it isn't and what it isn't doesn't actually exist because if everything that it isn't didn't exist then neither could the thing that we are trying to find out what it is!

Oh dear!

But what Einstein's theory says is that everything moves through the Universe in relation to everything else. And everything that exists, no matter how small it is, exerts a force on everything else and therefore influences everything else. (This is where we get what is called "The Butterfly Wing Effect" whereby a butterfly flapping its wings in South America can in effect cause a hurricane in North America simply by the law of compounding and aggregating effects.)

This also ties in what has come to known as The Big Bang Theory of the Universe in that it is believed that the whole Universe and everything thing in it is thought to have all emerged from a singular event approximately 13.7 billion years ago when something blew up or appeared out of nothing and nowhere and as it cooled down and expanded time, space and matter all began to appear. But all those things have the same point of origin and appearance and so they must have at some point all been the same thing.

Therefore, who is to say that they aren't still the same thing?

Now it could be argued that it is obvious that a rabbit isn't also Alpha Centauri. And at one level it clearly isn't because a rabbit happily hops around here on planet Earth whilst Alpha Centauri is a star that is millions of light years away and beyond our current technology to reach yet alone seek to claim that a rabbit and Alpha Centauri are one and the same thing.

But think about it for a moment inside the context of what is being said here. For by analogy is it any different to saying that a liver cell and a brain cell in the rabbit are part and parcel of the same creature?

If they were looked at on their own and in isolation, then it would be easy and indeed obvious to conclude that they were in no way related. But they are related for without both a brain and a liver, and countless other constituent parts, our rabbit wouldn't be able to exist.

It is only the distance of time and space (and differentiation) that makes us think that the realities of the rabbit and Alpha Centauri are separate and different. But without cell differentiation it would be impossible for a rabbit or any other animal, star, planet, moon or any other organic life to form up because the Universe would be made up entirely of one kind of cell.

But then again, maybe it is!

The Universe appears to be singular and multiple at the same time. And so therefore you must be too.

Again this appears to make sense for a human being is made up of billions of cells, multiple influences, and an unknown number of functions and processes going on simultaneously and goodness knows how many impressions when we walk down the street, most of which we are luckily unconscious of otherwise we would explode from sensory overload.

Which is why all forms of organic life within the Universe need to have a sense of coherence and context so that they can know what they are and what they aren't and therefore what their function is within the greater whole. This is why at the level of same but different the rabbit is at least unconsciously aware that it is not Alpha Centauri because it doesn't exhibit any of the characteristic behaviours that one would associate with a star in the sky. It somehow instinctively knows what a rabbit is and what a rabbit does and so it does those rabbit things whilst it remains in its rabbit coherent state.

Alpha Centauri on the other hand does not seem to exhibit signs or pretensions of being a rabbit. It doesn't have a fluffy tail, hop around and nor does it eat carrots for food.

And yet both are ultimately made up of the same "stuff".

It is only by distance that we can actually see what something is.
And also what it is not.
Which is partly why we have the saying – the heart of the matter can only be seen from afar.

But what about the converse of that saying which is – the afar of the matter can only be seen from the heart?

In other words, just what is it that has to look at something to see what its true nature is as opposed to the "stuff" that it is made of?

For whilst on the one hand we have electron microscopes to peer down into the world of the atom as mentioned earlier, we also have amazing telescopes with which we can now peer into the deep recesses of space and determine their very secrets.

Or can we?

Go to your bosom: Knock there, and ask your heart what it doth know.

William Shakespeare

We live today in what is often called the information age. This is especially so since the rise of the digital age and the invention of computers and the internet revolution. The amount of information available at the click of a finger is mind-blowingly quantum.

For it is now possible to store the complete works of the British Library on a few memory sticks that wouldn't even occupy the complete surface area of a computer desk, whereas the problem centuries ago was a very different one of firstly having access to an education that would enable one to be able to read and then getting access to the written word to find out about life and reality.

In fact, the problem centuries ago (and indeed still existent in the world today) was being allowed access to some of this information because not that long ago it was a punishable crime for the "ordinary" person to have their own copy of the Bible. People weren't allowed to read things for themselves because they might then start to think for themselves and that is the most dangerous thing in the world. So people were prevented from having access to controversial or seditious literature because it might challenge the conformity thinking and dogma of the day.

One only has to read the list of books banned by the Vatican in The *Index Librorum Prohibitorum* over the centuries to see that the suppression of freedom of thought has dogged the human story for many centuries.

For with people like Johannes Kepler, Jean-Paul Sartre, Simone de Beauvoir, Voltaire, Victor Hugo, Jean-Jacques Rousseau, Immanuel Kant, David Hume, René Descartes, Francis Bacon, John Milton, John Locke and Galileo Galilei on the list it was / is almost a badge of honour to be included. Hey maybe this book might make it too!

Of course that state of affairs still exists today and one doesn't have to look back that far in history to remember the book burnings carried out by the Nazis in the 1930's in an attempt to erase "impure" literature and knowledge.

We also have even today the struggle in many parts of the world for girls to even get access to any kind of education due to fundamentalist views that hold that girls being educated is a form of evil. These views are held to such an extreme level that teachers and the children themselves are regarded as being legitimate targets for assassination should they try and offer or receive such education.

This form of censorship seeks to suppress and eliminate anything that is different to the dogma or fundamentalism held by that which seeks to do the suppressing.

But today we have another form of censorship that exists in the information age and that is the censorship of there being very little or no censorship at all. It is a kind of reverse censorship for instead of finding a prevailing view or dogma that one isn't allowed to dissent from, one can now find every kind of view about every kind of subject from every kind of person. From scientific treatises to fundamentalist ventings to conspiracy theories of every shape and form that one could ever imagine and some that one could never even imagine in the first place!

It is almost therefore censorship by saturation. For how can one find out what one really thinks about something when one is bombarded on so many sides by what so many other people think about any particular given subject?

Perhaps this is where the quote from Shakespeare is so important?

Because in that quote what Shakespeare is referring to (even in his age of books being rare and special) is the fact that feeling is more important than thinking.

It is often said that a person only reads a newspaper to find out what their opinion is. To a large degree this is true, for the brain operates on a binary (by anagram binary anagrams to brainy) system of acceptance and rejection. Thus we either accept / reject, agree / disagree with the information we read or receive but mostly from a thinking or an opinion standpoint.

Yet in doing so we often neglect or ignore what we feel about the subject or matter in hand.

For Shakespeare is alluding to the fact that despite what we might think about it there is a part of us that already knows what it **feels** about it.

When we keep wondering what we think about something we take the heart out of the equation and move the process to the head and the brain. And as the brain is full of information the thinking process because one of linking to the information stored in their and so whatever is most powerful at any given moment then that is what we link to and so that is what we think!

This explains why it is hard to change one's opinion on the one hand (because the more one thinks something the more engraved that opinion becomes) and why on the other hand a person can suddenly change their mind out of the blue because that is literally what happens i.e. a new and better opinion appears and so one simply replaces the old opinion with the new one.

If such thinking and opinions are devoid of feeling then we do not open ourselves up to what we already know unconsciously. And what we know unconsciously is linked to much higher feelings than the exchange and mart of facts and opinions for it is governed by such things as empathy, care, compassion, kindness, humility, warmth, humanity and so on.

Facts and opinions come and go but feelings such as these are immortal and transcend time and space and indeed the sense of isolation and separateness we can all feel. They are interconnected as are we all. These are the things that join us, unite us and create the sense of togetherness and truth we share at a deeper, truly human and humane level.

These are the feelings of knowing what is right, what is true, what is natural and what it truly means to be human.

Yet we can suppress these natural feelings by drowning in a sea of information, facts, statistics, opinions and analysis. Especially when we keep asking ourselves and each other "What do you think?" as opposed to "What do you feel?"

For example, there is a world of difference between what one thinks about a sunset or a star filled sky at night and what one feels about it. All the information and facts in the world about these things cannot move a person or fill them with awe and wonder. But feelings can, and this is what they are meant to do.

It would seem that our feelings, emotions, instincts and sensings about things are much older than our ability to think about them in more abstract, philosophical and conceptual terms. Our feelings about things are more primordial and as such are less likely to be intellectual or abstract. This doesn't mean that they are always accurate or exact, but they are more likely to real.

Despite what they may tell you to the contrary, there is no book in the world that can give you the feeling of being in love. They may help remove some of the obstacles that get in the way of feeling the feeling of love but they don't give the person the feeling of itself. That feeling comes from within. And if it comes from within then it must have already been there. And if it is already there then it must have come from somewhere else in the first place. The question then is, where?

The only answer to that question is that too, like you, it must have come from somewhere else!

But perhaps not somewhere else in the way that we normally think of. For all the cells in the body come from somewhere else and in fact if you think about it you are in fact a completely different physical person than you were when you were born because each and every cell in your body has been replaced since that time. So if you ever get the feeling that you haven't been feeling yourself lately then that is probably because it's true!

This suggests that feelings and indeed thoughts aren't necessarily as physical as perhaps previously thought (or felt). There is a non local aspect to them that are held in the collective arrangement of the cells and the person and possibly in non local places such as the collective unconscious spoken of by Jung both in the individual and in the greater consciousness outside of the individual.

So feelings and thoughts just like the colour of one's hair, skin and eyes or the shape of one's nose can in fact be inherited or acquired from somewhere else.

This has to be true because one's beliefs, attitudes, opinions and values are acquired through one's life experience as we aren't born with them as we are born with a particular colour of skin or eyes.

We learn these things as we gather experience and develop our frames of reference through the course of our lives.

It is just as possible to inherit what we think as what we look like which is a rather scary thought! But feelings are different for as stated previously they are much more primal and visceral and therefore more likely to be both original and individual.

However, with the rise of civilisation and in particular the movement away from feelings to thinking as accelerated by the Renaissance and the so called Age of Enlightenment this led to an increasing sense of moving the human centre of gravity from the heart to the head. For without this shift there wouldn't have been a change in polarity that would have allowed the Industrial Revolution to occur and nor could there be such a sense of separateness and seeing things as things rather than as processes unto themselves.

This has occurred to such a degree that we now mostly see the Earth and Nature as things that are separate to ourselves, rather than feeling ourselves to be a part of them, integrated with them and totally connected to them in the way that most so called primitive tribes of the world still do.

For having that intimacy of feeling wouldn't allow one to pollute, plunder and destroy the very ecology that one is part of in the first place. It would be totally alien and antithetical to that feeling and would be akin to poisoning oneself, which is in fact what a lot of people now do when one considers what they eat, drink, breathe and even think.

There is a great deal of difference between information and knowledge, and modern living has given people access to an incredible amount of information, but possibly at the expense of knowledge or perhaps what might be better termed natural wisdom.

Ancient people didn't have access to computers, the internet or chat rooms, but they did have a vast knowledge of nature and its processes. Perhaps that is why they felt things about nature and the planet that we modern humans easily dismiss as superstitious nonsense and mythology. Yet they came out of their feelings about their experiences and so we need to be careful not to judge those feelings with modern day thoughts. For if the boot, or bare foot were the other way round then how would they judge or assess our so called modern successes of over crowded and polluted cities, rivers and air?

It is easy to rationalise and justify what one does through the thinking process because there is always more than one way to think about something. But it is not so easy to change what one feels about something. What it is possible to do is to suppress those feelings by giving greater credence and importance and amperage to what one thinks as opposed to what one feels.

Shakespeare is pointing us all to the part of ourselves that knows.

But the only way that the heart will tell us the answer is if we ask it.

And if we ask it what it and what we feel.

Non-violence is not a garment to be put on and off at will. Its seat is in the heart, and it must be an inseparable part of our being.

Mahatma Gandhi

The principle of non-violence was a central tenet within the philosophy of Mahatma Gandhi throughout his life in seeking to change oppression and suppression wherever he met it.

In his view if he met violence with violence then what real change would he in fact be proposing from the pre-existing order that used violence in order to maintain power and control over that which is suppressed?

As he himself often said – an eye for an eye soon leaves everybody blind.

The curious thing about non-violence is that there is no actual word in English for it as a positive attribute. Our reference for it takes it as being the state of **non** violence. It's almost as though all the violence that existed before the state of non violence arrived has been removed and taken away by the negation or removal of permission for violence to exist in that particular time and space.

Non-violence isn't pacifism and nor is it peace. Peace is obviously a state where violence is absent but the concept of non-violence implies an active state of some kind whereas peace is where that state has arrived and is present and it exists by and of its own account. And pacifism doesn't convey what non-violence is either for it is more to do with a stance, an attitude and a state of mind, whereas non-violence is more active in its expression.

The fact of the absence of a proactive word for non-violence says quite a lot about our modern societies and how they are configured, constructed and reinforced and changed. Because usually when they are changed it is because of revolution as opposed to evolution i.e. they are overthrown. Even in what we in the West might call our peaceful democracies changes of government have their own forms of violence. For every time there is an election and the people vote for a change then the previous administration is thrown out of office and the new administration comes into power in triumph and proceeds to change what the previous government did to what they want to do.

And the previous government changes from being the ruling power base to literally being the Opposition, which when you think about it is a fairly violent default starter position from which to begin. It states that whatever you, the ruling party are for, we are against as a matter of fundamental principle unless there are very good reasons for us not to be against you!

Now admittedly this doesn't usually operate at the level physical violence, although sometimes it does, but nevertheless it does carry its own level of subtle violence because it is based in an adversarial process. And this adversarial stance is enforced within the "opposition" process because the parties in power and in opposition have a whip system which literally means that the individual within the party has to toe the party line on any given issue to ensure that a united front of opposition is maintained.

If the individual refuses to follow the party line, then they themselves will also be subjected to violence and they will be given the "whip" i.e. punished in some shape or form for voting with their conscience or moral code. This can involve anything from rebuke, to demotion, to exclusion from the party.

Yet from the voter's standpoint the very reason why they voted the candidate into power in their constituency was so that they would follow their conscience and moral code. There is therefore a massive contradiction within the whole whip process.

And so the candidate has to decide on whether they want to be included within the due political process or be banned from it and thereby marginalised and excluded.

Most of course do follow the party line and end up getting ahead according to the principle espoused by Sir Joseph Porter in the Gilbert and Sullivan opera HMS Pinafore.

Sir Joseph: *I grew so rich that I was sent*
By a pocket borough into Parliament.
I always voted at my party's call,
And I never thought of thinking for myself at all.
I thought so little, they rewarded me
By making me the Ruler of the Queen's Navee!

CHORUS. — *He thought so little, they rewarded him*
By making him the Ruler of the Queen's Navee!

Quite!

So if a person isn't thinking for themselves then clearly someone or something else is doing the thinking for them and that of itself is a form of invasion and therefore in its own way a form of violence. A bit like the line in Dark

Side of the Moon: *"There's someone in my head but it's not me."*

Who put those thoughts, ideas, beliefs, dogmas, fundamentalisms, brain-washings and so much more in there without my permission?

Given this permanent state of affairs of being assaulted on every side by being told what and how to think about everything no wonder it is sometimes said that the hardest thing in the world is to think for oneself.

For before one can think for oneself one has to first get rid of everything that everyone else has put in there with or without the person's knowledge or consent.

But how does a person get rid of these invasive views and opinions in a non-violent way, especially when there isn't a proactive word that expresses the action of non-violence without the prefix non?

Ghandi himself struggled with this concept and tried to come up with a new word to replace non-violence. In the end he settled for the word SATYAGRAHA which takes it root meaning from the word satya which means truth. So to Ghandi the word Satyagraha meant *"holding on to truth"* or at a more esoteric level it represented a *"truth force"*.

This is much more than the concept of non-violence for it involves an energy and a state and a stance and an action. That process is based around the notion of doing so on behalf of something else, which in this context is the truth. For if something is the truth then it can't have violence attached to it because truth is never violent. It can be extremely powerful and in fact always is, but it of itself is never violent as such.

It may appear to be violent, such as perhaps in the event of things such as earthquakes and volcanoes but at a deeper level within the truth of these actions there is a creative force at play that brings new life and new opportunities.

Yet strangely despite the beauty of the word and its meaning it has never caught on in popular parlance. And in its stead we are left with the lesser potent view of non-violence whereas in actual fact it was much deeper than that.

That having been said, why does Ghandi say that the seat of non-violence is in the heart? Why is it not in the head, or the mind, or the big toe for that matter? What is it about the heart that makes it suitable home for non-violence and a fortress for its deeper meaning which is the truth?

Perhaps it is something to do with the nature of the heart itself in that it pumps out the very life force itself that keeps each and every one of us alive? For without its life affirming action of beating on average over 100,000 times a day for each and every person on Earth then none of us would in fact be alive to wonder about non-violence or anything else for that matter. Each time the heart beats it forces the blood in the arties to each and every cell in the body and carries with it oxygen and nutriment.

In one sense even the action of the heart itself could at one level be regarded as being "violent" for its pumping action is very intense and has to carry a great force with it in order to reach each and every cell. It is also pretty relentless in its action because if it wasn't then that would mean the end of life for us all.

Yet it clearly isn't a violent action at all at core because it carries the life affirming force that keeps us alive as long as it continues to beat.

The *"truth force"* that Ghandi was trying to encapsulate when he used the word Satyagraha represents the higher case where non-violence is concerned. It is clearly beyond pacifism because in no way can it be said that the heart is passive in its function, action and purpose.

It was this force the British met when Ghandi decided to make his mark by stating that the people would go and collect salt. They refused to engage in violence and simply walked to the shore to collect the salt that they needed. Of course this was a symbolic gesture because in collecting the salt they were in fact challenging British authority because as far as they were concerned the salt was British property and by seeking to collect it the Indians were seeking to usurp that authority.

Therefore, to reinforce that control the British met this non-violent action with violence to suppress the protest.

But since the violence was met with none in return it became impossible to justify the violence that was inflicted on the people. Thus its power base or mandate was removed and slowly the tide turned towards independence from their colonial masters for the Indian people and they then became free to gather their salt in peace.

It is a truth that violence never stops violence but simply perpetuates it in either the same of another form. For just as energy cannot be created or destroyed nor can violence. But it can be avoided, for always there is another path and Ghandi was saying was that that path lies in and from the heart.

For true and genuine feelings emanate from the heart and it is a place where hatred, envy, deceit, control, selfishness and greed cannot reside. It is not like a garment that can be put on or taken off or comes into and goes out of fashion. It is indelible and part of our being when we are consumed by our doing.

It is part of our spiritual DNA, the refined and the ineffable, unnameable thing that makes us who and what we really are. The place that lives beyond fear and insecurity.

And that true place of Satyagraha is known also by another name and that is love.

For love is never violent. For if it was then it wouldn't and couldn't be love.

It gives without counting the cost and then gives some more and forgives the error and offers more love in return.

When Jesus Christ said that if your enemy strikes you on the cheek, turn the other cheek, he was espousing exactly the same principle as Ghandi which is:

Open up your heart and let the sunshine in (and out).

Once I knew only darkness and stillness... my life was without past or future... but a little word from the fingers of another fell into my hand that clutched at emptiness, and my heart leaped to the rapture of living.

Helen Keller

When I was growing up in the 1960's Helen Keller was one of my absolute heroes. I think I first heard about her life and her story from reading those pocket editions of Readers Digest that we used to get every month or so.

Her life was truly a remarkable one, and I felt both humbled and inspired in equal measure to read about her journey out from darkness into light as she describes so beautifully above.

For those who don't know Helen Keller, she was born in Alabama to a reasonably well off family in 1880. She was born a perfectly normal, healthy and happy child but when she was about 19 months old she developed a fever (possibly scarlet fever or meningitis). As a result of contracting this fever she lost both her eyesight and her hearing and although she still had the faculty of her voice, to all intents and purposes she was also struck dumb for she was only at that age just learning language and the ability to communicate through words and sentences.

This was an absolutely debilitating life changing event for her as her world disappeared from being one of light and a cacophony of sounds into one of no sound and no light.

A prison to which it seemed she had been sentenced for life with no chance of remission.

This sudden change obviously frustrated the little girl very much indeed, and she and her family found it very difficult if not nearly impossible to communicate with each other.

In 1886 when Helen was about 6 years old she was introduced to Anne Sullivan, a young teacher who was asked to try and help Helen in her situation. Anne herself was visually impaired and at the time when they first met in 1886 was only 20 years old.

This meeting however was to change both their lives forever, because not only did Anne become Helen's teacher and later governess, but she also became her life long friend for the next 49 years until Anne died.

When they first met, although Helen could communicate very basic concepts and needs through signing she had very little interaction with people and had retreated very much back into her shell and was prone to throwing lots of tantrums and screaming sometimes for hours on end.

When Anne came into her life that all began to change as Anne showed Helen a tremendous amount of love, patience and understanding as they tried to find a way to cross the divide between light and dark where both could meet in the light.

Initially they were not able to establish a link as Anne would place a doll in Helen's hand and then spell out the word D-O-L-L into Helen's hand so she would hopefully know what it was in fact that she was holding.

It was only when Anne placed some water in Helen's hand and then spelt out the word W-A-T-E-R that Helen had a eureka moment and realised what was happening and the connection between the object and the "sign". Helen later described this as literally like a light being switched on in her previously dark world. She also described how she felt her heart leap at suddenly no longer being so alone, so isolated, so lost.

From that moment on Helen, with Annie's help was able to learn how to communicate from inside her world to the outside world and she could also know find a way to understand, again with Annie's help, what the outside world was like and what it might want to say to her.

It was as if in 1886 two destinies met, for although it is fairly obvious to see that Helen needed Annie to help her find out her way, in some way Annie also needed Helen because Helen's need brought out the very best in the humanity and skill that Annie had to offer. Later in life it became much more of an equal partnership where both needed each other for support, companionship and friendship.

When Annie got older she became more or less totally blind and when she died it was Helen who was holding her hand when she passed away. What an incredibly moving moment as for over the previous 49 years their two hands had been Helen's primary source of communicating with the outside world.

Therefore, Helen Keller is indeed a superbly qualified person to speak of matters of the heart.

Her hauntingly beautiful quote speaks of a heart being unlocked and opened to what she calls the rapture of living. And for her it no doubt was precisely like that because she could now "see" in a way that she previously couldn't. Suddenly so much more was possible and at the same time so much less was impossible.

Helen had been set free in ways that many people who have the gift of sight and speech aren't. For she never took her gifts for granted and she was never familiar with them or her life and she sought to develop them in whatever way possible. She became famous and travelled widely giving talks and lectures and encouraging and championing those who may have been dealt a difficult hand in life.

She was a shining example of that which she espoused for others.

Helen is remembered as an advocate for people with disabilities, but she was also involved in numerous other causes. She was among other things a suffragist, a pacifist, a radical socialist and a birth control supporter.

In 1915 she and George Kessler founded the Helen Keller International (HKI) organization. This organization is devoted to research into vision, health and nutrition.

In 1920 she helped to found the American Civil Liberties Union which is still very much active today in helping the under-privileged and the disenfranchised.

Whatever opened Helen Keller's heart that day in 1886 allowed a tremendous amount of humanity, kindness, passion, compassion, hope, inspiration and love to pour forth. Perhaps the key was in Annie knocking on the door and asking if anyone was home. And with the right amount of care, patience and warmth both Annie and Helen found that there was indeed someone living in Helen's heart and they were both surprised who it was.

To one degree or another all suffer the pain of being in prison and locked away from who they really are and what they really feel. General life experience, familiarity and taking things for granted can dull the senses and feelings down due to the pressure of conformity and expectancies of how one should behave.

Our behaviours adapt according to our experiences and we find roles that enable us to fit in to society, but at what price to our sensitivities? It is clear that our sensitivities become dulled down because compared to so called primitive people our sensitivities of sound, smell, touch, taste and hearing are quite poor. Those who live in nature have a much more acute sense in these faculties.

The saying that goes with this is – if you don't use it you lose it. Or perhaps if you don't use it to the fullest then you won't get the best return out of it, or it might even give you false information if you are not careful. For example, it might deceive you into thinking that a giant concrete carbuncle is somehow a work of art or that artificial scents are in fact beautiful or that food laced with preservatives and additives actually tastes delicious.

Our senses were developed to keep us safe and healthy, and they are our road map through life but if we become separated from them then our navigation system goes seriously awry and we can be tricked by false gods and signals.

Perhaps this is what Shakespeare was alluding to when he wrote the following about the five wits:

The five wits were:

Common Sense

Memory
Estimation
Imagination
Fantasie

These were seen as a whole development and education process for they measured the mark of a true man (or a woman). They are probably linked to the five senses (sight, sound, touch, taste and smell) for who can truly be wise without relying on the heightened use of their sensory faculties?

Indeed, at the time of Shakespeare the five wits were regarded as being the inward wits whereas the five senses were considered as being the outward wits.

He refers to them on several occasions in his plays and sonnets for example:

"Thou hast more of the wild goose in one of they wits – than 1 have in my whole five."
Romeo and Juliet

"Four of his five wits went halting off, and now is the whole man governed with one."
Much Ado about Nothing

and

"But my five wits not my sense can Dissuade one foolish heart from serving thee."
Sonnet 141

Yet wisdom doesn't just come from the use of those five outer faculties alone as Helen Keller demonstrably proved. For she showed that the switching on of the inner wits wasn't dependant on all the outer wits working fully or at all.

All that was needed was an open heart and a love and a compassion for her fellow human beings for something to come shining out from her heart like a beacon of light and hope.

I certainly remember having that kind of feeling when I became fascinated by her life and journey when I first read about her when I was ten years old. I remember thinking that I somehow wanted my life to shine as brightly as hers shone into mine. The feeling I got was one that anything is possible if you try your best and if you don't let what you or anybody else thinks stop you doing so.

These thoughts and feelings weren't academic at all for they were visceral. I could feel them in my being and not only that, but they were throughout.

Of course I am sure that Helen Keller wasn't perfect or a saint and that she no doubt had her faults as we all do. But there was a feeling that there was something perfect about the qualities that lived with her and came through her life. It wasn't as though these feelings were strange or completely new, because I recognised them somehow. They felt familiar, warm, accepting and welcoming. They were comforting to be with and they felt safe, secure and radiant.

There is something about overcoming adversity that allows something else to come through a life because of what has been earned and won in the endeavour of trying. It defies the easy come easy go attitude that so devalues the true worth of things especially in our instant gratification, throw away society that commoditises and cheapens things.

Helen Keller took her greatest pleasures from the smallest and simplest things. And that taught my life a lesson of not taking things for granted.

What greater demonstration of the power of the heart can there be than holding the hand of your teacher, friend and life long companion as they pass from this life to the next? Especially when that hand is the hand with which you told the world what you thought, felt, loved and cared about from the very core of your being.

How incredibly profound and intimate and deeply moving.

How truly religious in the simplest, kindest non-intellectual way possible.

God may or may not live in a church, temple, mosque or synagogue.

But if there is a God then he, she or it is much more likely to live in holding of the hand of another and at the same time holding the best of them whilst giving them all the love you have in your heart by saying:

"Thank you from the bottom of my heart."

If you look into your own heart, and you find nothing wrong there, what is there to worry about? What is there to fear?

Confucius

Our modern world is a very easy place to find oneself to be confused, uncertain and insecure. There are so many diverse things and needs that all require our attention and the speed of life today is so fast that it is very easy to make a mistake, get things wrong or make a faux pas or cringe-worthy social gaffe by wearing the wrong lipstick or perhaps the wrong shoes with a suit.

We worry and stress about a lot stuff that in the big scheme of things really matter very little if in fact they even matter at all. There is a huge pressure to be a certain way, think a certain way, follow fashion and of course fit in in a particular way.

The world preys on our doubts and insecurities and does this so that it can persuade us that we need things that we don't have that will somehow make us feel more secure and therefore fit in better. We are trained to doubt ourselves and listen to those we think know us better than we know ourselves, and so they can tell us what we need so that we can with their help know and be ourselves better than we could be if we were just left alone!

Always there is some kind of external criteria measuring the truth, merit and validity of what we think, what we do and what we believe from the fashion police, to the courts of law and justice to peer group pressure and societal norms and conformities.

And you'd jolly well better get it right, because if you don't someone somewhere might just slap some kind of exclusion or punishment order upon you.

No wonder we worry and stress a lot therefore, because we are always thinking that the measurement of truth and merit is outside of ourselves. That someone or something else will be the judge and jury of who we are and what we do.

Even worse, sometimes we ourselves join this judge and jury bandwagon in passing critical judgements on ourselves and then executing punishment by beating ourselves up and even most sadly of all some can take this to an extreme level by deciding that life is no longer worth living and take their own life.

For this to occur there has to be a huge disconnection from what the person actually is and represents as a human being, and what they **think** they are and represent or don't as the case may be. For a person to think that life is no longer worth living they are clearly at distance from the gift of life and all that offers, sometimes through no fault of their own because the outer life often makes people feel that there is little point in trying to go on because they don't feel they fit in or have anything useful or meaningful to offer others or themselves.

Just like much of the food we eat isn't good for us with all the artificial things put in it and the processing that may be dome to it, then so it is with the impressions we are also forced to consume from advertising to newspapers, to television to education and so much more.

Our senses are assailed to such a degree that sometimes we simply can't take any more, and they and we then tend to shut down to try and make an effort to cope with the assault.

What Confucius is saying here is that inside all the outer noise there is a quiet place inside where one can begin to find the truth of oneself and who and what one really is and why we do what we do.

A place that doesn't lie, for either the heart beats the next beat or it doesn't. It can't pretend to do it because if it did we would soon know about it!

The heart itself isn't governed by fear, but its workings are certainly affected by fear and it reacts accordingly by working harder and pumping the blood and adrenalin around the body so that we can deal with the situation that is causing us to be fearful.

Usually the response to fear is fight or flight, but really what is it that we are fighting or running away from? Usually in fact it is ourselves and who and what we really are. For there has to be something seriously wrong with the world when people say that the thing they fear most is not death or torture but public speaking! The fear of speaking in front of other people is greater than life itself ending. This is clearly bizarre in the extreme.

The maxim expressed by the oracle at Delphi was – Know Thyself. This is an apparently simple statement, but it requires a huge amount of knowledge and personal development to understand and appreciate it fully or even partially. For beyond the superficiality of name, gender, job and identity what does it really mean to know oneself at a very deep level?

What is the true thyself of the self? When all that isn't
the self of the self is stripped away who and what is left
there in the core of the being of the person?

To know thyself is to know no fear of the self. For what
is the point of running away from oneself when the bits
that one is running away from are running just as fast in
the same direction?

Or to fight those things in oneself that one doesn't like?
There is no point because they cannot be defeated. But
if one knows oneself then they can be accepted and not
judged.

This is the place from which fear begins to retreat.
For that which can accept the truth doesn't try and
change it into a lesser truth or a falsehood.

As Mark Twain once said: *"Tell no lies and then you have
nothing to remember."*

Imagine the stress that a compulsive liar puts their body
under by having to remember which lies were told to
which person on what date and why. The amount of
toxic baggage that this person carries around in their
system is horrendous. And it is toxic in its nature
because telling lies isn't natural and has the exact same
effect as eating poisonous foods for that is what it
actually is, unnatural food.

Telling lies puts the human system into contradiction
and this has the effect of tying up the physical, mental
and emotional systems into knots and prevents them
from working efficiently and effectively. It's a bit like
what happens when one takes a hose that has a good
flow of water running through it and then bending the
hose somewhere along its length. Once this is done the

flow of water is blocked off completely or at least it slows down to a mere trickle.

Lying has this affect on the person, plus of course the effect that is has on the people who are being told the lie for it can only damage them too.

It is quite extraordinary when one considers it, just how often people when they are faced with a difficult problem or an event where they have clearly done wrong or made a mistake, immediately consider what kind of fabricated story or excuse they can make up so that they can get away with it or not have to admit that they have messed up, apologise, seek forgiveness and then try and move on.

Sometimes the truth is seen as the worst option or not one worth considering.

But considering that it was a truth that led to the person getting themselves into the current state of affairs that they find themselves in, then surely the truth is the best way to try and get themselves out of it? For Occam's Razor states that the simplest solution is always the easiest and most viable and most preferred by nature, for the more complicated the method or proposed solution then the less likely it is to be selected.

Given the fact that telling lies is far more complicated than telling the truth (for think of the amount of energy it requires to make up a fabricated story rather than telling the truth and then remembering who you told what to) you would probably think that people would prefer to tell the truth and save time, energy and most importantly of all relationships by making admission and seeking to put things right and be forgiven.

But no, mostly people seek to preserve their perceived image and save face in any way that they can and hope that the lies do not get discovered (at least by the parties in receipt of them).

It is said that one can hide lies but you can't hide the truth for it has to go somewhere. And if the truth doesn't go to where it should go i.e. the third party, then it has only one place left to go and that is internally inside the person who is telling the lie.

And once it goes in there it meets its antithesis because inside the person is another version of the same set of events i.e. the lie.

When the truth meets the lie there can only be conflict and effectively by harbouring both the truth and lie about the same event inside themselves the person to all intents and purposes declares war on themselves. And we all know this to be true because when we lie we go into contortions and angst about it, stress out, have trouble sleeping, wrestle with the possible consequences of being found to be liar, feel guilty about what it might be doing to the party who has been lied to and so on and so on.

It is clearly therefore far more economical to tell the truth. It's also simpler, cleaner and more natural and is a better bet for the future where evolutionary theory is concerned.

This is what Confucius is referring to in his quote.

If a person looks in to their heart and finds that they have done nothing wrong what is there to worry about?

This doesn't mean that people should be perfect or that they shouldn't make mistakes, or that they don't hurt other people in some way. These things we all do to some degree or another.

What it means however is that when a person looks inside their heart to see what the truth is then they find that at that point in time they have done all they possibly can do to make matters, right, true, just and fair.

If they have done something hurtful then it's not just enough to admit that they have done it, they need to try to put matters right. And if in looking into their heart they see that there is more that they could do and should do to correct the error then this will happily do because that is what the truth does.

It seeks to preserve and restore the truth to all parties involved and not just the person who may have done wrong and wishes to bring themselves back in to balance. For it is not possible to bring oneself back in to balance without bringing back in to balance (as best as one can) all the other parties that one may have unbalanced in the first place by what one did.

One ought to hold on to one's heart; for if one lets it go, one soon loses control of the head too.

Friedrich Nietzsche

Friedrich Nietzsche was a German philosopher, poet and composer who lived in the 19th century. He wrote on many diverse subjects including religion, morality, contemporary culture, philosophy and science. The breadth and range of topics he covered in his writing was truly extraordinary but perhaps could best be summed up as journeys into the meaning of life.

A central tenet within his writing was the assertion that any true meaning to life had to be somehow confirmed within what he termed *"life affirmation"*. This meant that unless the philosophy or meaning was acquired out of real life experiences for the person then it was both intellectual and dangerous. He very much warned against the following of dogmas and conformities and considered that a person needed to follow their own path, their own conscience, their own truth and most importantly of all what their own experience told them was real and meaningful.

Otherwise a person was doomed to a life of following the dogmas and truths of others, be they church or state institutions, politicians, friends and family and even philosophers!

Because unless a person had real life experiences of what they believed then they had no way of measuring the veracity or truth of what they had adopted. And no matter how esteemed or popular the view they were following was, without personal confirmation of its accuracy and applicability then it could only be opinion.

For a person to follow another's truth is tantamount to not living at all. Far better to be alone and true to one's own experience and beliefs than to be a sheep in amongst the flock and following the shepherd's every beck and call.

It has to be said that that living on the edge of this twilight zone between conformity and freedom cost Nietzsche his own sanity for he suffered a complete mental collapse in 1889 from which he never really recovered before his death in 1900.

The struggle to be free is never an easy one which is perhaps why so few people attempt to do it in any real, meaningful or deep way and instead settle for lives of conformity and mediocrity. They end up living lives that Thoreau described as ones of quiet desperation.

It seems that in his pursuit of higher consciousness Nietzsche was not himself able to keep his feet on the ground, and therefore he suffered for his art and his search for truth.

He is reputed to be the originator of the phrase *God is Dead* (it appears in a several of his works including Thus Spoke Zarathustra) and many have since interpreted that phrase as meaning that Nietzsche was an atheist.

But this is to take what he was saying out of context and thus twist the meaning. Ironically he gives a fuller explanation of what he meant in the writing *"The Madman"* which appears in the book The Gay Science in 1882 just seven years before his own collapse.

The relevant passage reads as follows:

"God is dead. God remains dead. And we have killed him. Yet his shadow still looms. How shall we comfort ourselves, the murderers of all murderers? What was holiest and mightiest of all that the world has yet owned has bled to death under our knives: who will wipe this blood off us? What water is there for us to clean ourselves? What festivals of atonement, what sacred games shall we have to invent? Is not the greatness of this deed too great for us? Must we ourselves not become gods simply to appear worthy of it?"

It is clear from this passage that Nietzsche isn't proclaiming that he is an atheist, but rather stating that the way the human race has treated God (sometimes in the name of God himself) shows that in fact the human race has killed the true idea of who and what God really is and begun to worship false gods instead, i.e. themselves.

Perhaps this is what Nietzsche is referring to when he talks about the relationship between the heart and the head in the quote?

For if what one feels in the heart is denied or abandoned then the head can certainly come up with some very funny ideas indeed.

The story that comes to mind where this is concerned is that of Icarus who in Greek mythology in seeking to escape from Crete made himself some wings so he could simply fly away to the mainland as the birds did. However, in doing so he ignored the advice he was given and he flew too close to the Sun and this caused the wax in his wings to melt and so he crashed in to the sea and was drowned.

The story is seen quite obviously as an example of the consequences of human hubris or failed ambition and also is a warning against rising above one's station or proven abilities and counsels against getting too big for one's boots. In other words, in modern parlance it warns against believing too much in one's own PR.

The Romans sought to address this propensity for ego inflation by ensuring that when an all conquering emperor or general returned home to Rome to a tumultuous welcome there was always on the parade someone like a slave whispering in the general or emperor's ear throughout the parade: *"Remember you are not a god you are just a man."*

The evidence of history suggests that many if not most of the emperors and generals must have been hard of hearing!

For if one somehow gets in to one's head that one is a god, guru, master, genius or hero (and then gets a lot of other people to confirm this theory) then it is very hard to get rid of that idea no matter what evidence to the contrary is presented.

This condition is not at all a rare one in human history with many cultures from all around the world throughout the ages all seeking to humanise god through the agency of a particular person known variously as the king, the emperor, the pharaoh, and perhaps even the Pope (when for example he declares himself to be infallible on any given issue).

Just in case a person may think that this infallibility is an old, non longer invoked "right" the last time it was declared was as recent as 1950 when Pope Pius the 12th stated that it was an infallible article of faith and truth that Mary the mother of Jesus didn't die a physical death but was assumed in to heaven completely intact in human bodily form.

There is no first hand evidence of this "fact" or proof that it happened, but that apparently doesn't matter because the Pope can claim supremacy over all matters spiritual should the powers invested in him as supreme pontiff need him to do so.

This "infallibility" goes back centuries to things like the Dictatus Papae which states that *"The Roman church has never erred; nor will it err to all eternity, the Scripture bearing witness*"

So that would appear to be that then.

Of course this one exercise of assumed supreme power could be exampled countless times throughout world history from the idea of the God king or Pharaoh in Ancient Egypt to the divine rights of kings in the middle ages to the suppression of religious expression in the communist era by the anti god gods of people like Stalin and Chairman Mao to the Pol Pot regime in Cambodia to the modern day gods of money and consumerism and all who worship at their altars.

Just because someone doesn't believe in God doesn't mean that they don't serve and worship one.

This is perhaps again what Nietzsche is warning against in respect of the relationship between the heart and the head.

The head can have great ideas but they need to be grounded in a greater reality of feelings and humility.

Perhaps a clue lies in the fact that Earth anagrams to Heart?

It is also significant that the earth wire in an electrical circuit provides the safety that prevents the circuit from exploding if the positive and negative wires connect. In order to perform this function, the earth wire needs to be neutral.

It is hard for people to stay neutral inside the experiences that happen in a life because we are so trained to judge everything in terms of good or bad, happy or sad, like or dislike and so on. By doing this we end up placing ourselves in the centre of every experience had and thereby inevitably develop either a superiority or inferiority complex and /or both and easily shift between the two according to what happens to us and how we interpret those events in our lives through our various filters.

It is interesting that we have the expression when someone has an ego flare about some success that *"It has gone to his / her head."* Or that someone has developed a big head which means the same thing.

We don't say that something has gone to someone's heart or that they have developed a big heart. In fact, if we say that someone has a big heart it means that they are the complete opposite of ego driven and that they are kind, warm, generous, compassionate and humble. Also we say that someone has taken something to heart, which means they have accepted and embraced something at a deep level.

This therefore suggests that modern living has become much more head dominated in its processes, and this has developed a dangerous tendency to let ideas run away with themselves before checking with the heart how they feel and how they relate to the greater context, the bigger picture, and to a more holistic and integrated view of reality.

The head might think that nuclear weapons are a good idea for national security but the heart would never do so. The head might say that the offender needs to be punished for the crime but the heart would always look to restore the injured and heal the wound. The head would tend to think the end justifies the means and that the focus is always on the desired result or outcome whereas the heart would say that it is the process that matters every time. For the process is the end as the two cannot be divorced in such a clinical way.

The head could say that nature is a thing to be controlled and used according to our need and pleasure whereas the heart would say that there is no such thing as "over there" or some kind of pecking order within nature where some things have superior rights and needs over others. The head might say that animals for example don't have rights or feel pain in the same way that human beings do, but the heart would know that they have the same rights as we do and they most certainly do feel pain.

The heart will know when something is wrong, whereas the head might think that it is not, especially when it manages to persuade others to its point of view. The head can rationalise and explain things away which is why we have things like murder, rape, torture, war, genocide, pollution, deforestation and so on in the world. For these things to occur someone, somewhere must have persuaded themselves and others that these actions were justified when clearly they are not.

That is why it is important to look inside one's heart and find out what is really there.

One only has to listen to the constant rhythm and beating of the heart and know that the very thing that keeps the truth of you alive will always tell you what you need to know and be if only you ask it and then listen for and to the answer.

The heart has its reasons of which reason knows nothing.

Blaise Pascal

At first glance this quote from Pascal makes no sense at all, for how can reasons not make sense to reason? One would think that the first thing to understand reason would be reason itself for otherwise the fact that reasons don't make sense to reason makes those reasons .... well, unreasonable!

Yet at another level we know exactly what Pascal is referring to here because real life doesn't move in linear ways of grids and fixed patterns, despite rigorous attempts by the outer world to make it like that with timetables, schedules, work, routines, habits, clocks and so on.

A bit like the lines of the limerick that go:

> *There once was a man who said damn,*
> *It appears to me now that I am*
> *Just a being that moves*
> *In pre-destinate groves*
> *In fact, not a bus but a tram.*

In other words, mostly our lives are governed by external forces that are beyond our control and any idea that we have real choice or freedom is badly mistaken because it is all decided and pre-determined in the way that a tram can only move down the tracks on which it runs and isn't free to go anywhere outside those pre-set tramlines.

Free will is a nice idea but really it is no more than that, a nice idea.

Before dismissing this assertion as being outlandish and not the case, it is important to state that in fact this thesis lies at the heart of Darwinism and particularly within Neo-Darwinism. For this asserts that we are almost slaves of our genes and there is nothing much we can do about this because it is the genes that are the driver and not ourselves. Some Neo-Darwinists even assert that the reason why we exist is so that we can carry genes around so that they can be carried forward into future generations via the process of natural selection.

We therefore exist for our genes and not the other way around!

The mechanisms of nature (for that is how Neo Darwinism views nature as being a largely, if not fully mechanical process) are pre-set and cannot be changed. Therefore, everything a person thinks and does is driven by this automatic and robotic process and all decisions and actions are governed by the need of the genes to continue into the future.

Whether or not this theory about being controlled by our genes is true or not it makes for a cold, heartless and unappealing world. For all a person's hopes, fears, loves, feelings, emotions and passions are all governed by the ghost in the machine and not themselves. And anyway the person isn't really themselves for in effect they are in reality a gene carrying automaton.

These views are of course extreme, but they are given a lot of credence in modern evolutionary and scientific circles. Especially with the rise of science and its ever increasing ability to develop more and more sophisticated technologies to peer into the workings of nature and life and see the processes by which it works, or at least how it apparently works.

Charles Darwin came up with the theory of natural selection in the middle of the 19th century and to say that his theory turned the world on its head would be a massive understatement because up until that time Creationism (the theory that God made things as they are and that humans were superior and set apart from the rest of nature) held sway in most people's minds.

Darwin showed that this wasn't the case and that species evolved over long periods of time and that via natural selection those species with the most advantageous adaptations were more likely to survive than those without them. And this process was an ongoing and dynamic one as environments and species evolved.

This quickly became known as a process of survival of the fittest. The perception became established, and was held by Darwin himself, that life is a jungle and it's a dog eat dog battle out there in the contest of life, and that only the strong survive and the weak become eliminated.

In fact, Darwin himself became subject to his own theory because he allegedly came up with his theory over 20 years before it was published, but didn't want to publish it because of the furore he knew it would trigger. But then Alfred Russell Wallace, who had been doing his own completely independent studies and research, came up with the same theory. He sent Darwin a copy of his paper on the subject for Darwin's thoughts and comments before planning to send it to the Royal Society.

Darwin then went into a fit of panic because he thought he was going to be cheated of the credit for his big idea. He then began to hatch a scheme with his friends that would ensure that he and not Wallace was going to be the main proponent of the theory, and history records that to be the case because who knows of Wallace's evolutionary theory today? Very few.

Darwin proved himself to be the better competitor, and so the theory of evolution carries his DNA and genes and not those of Wallace.

What is fascinating about the matter however, is the different emphases of the two approaches within the theory.

Darwin placed a much greater emphasis on the competitive side of the process i.e. only the strong or best adapted survive whereas Wallace saw it more in terms of the least well adapted not going forward.

Darwin therefore saw the garden as a jungle and it was a constant battle to survive whereas Wallace saw it as more of a constant process of refinement and improvement where species evolve to meet new needs and new requirements. Wallace saw things in a more holistic and integrated way, where species evolve together rather than just compete and so in that way he was on the early path to seeing things in a bigger context as put forward by James Lovelock in his Gaia hypothesis nearly 100 years later.

So the same theory, but with very different emphasis within the two approaches. As we now know, it is Darwin's version that has survived and has dominated evolutionary thinking for 150 years. And not just evolutionary thinking but social, political and economic thinking as well in ways that have often be self-serving, deterministic and at times appallingly inhuman.

This is not to blame Darwin in any way for having a theory, because a theory is a theory and only that. It is the interpretation of the theory and putting that interpretation into practice that matters, and many since Darwin have misinterpreted the process of evolution to suit their own ends and purposes.

But the phrase – survival of the fittest - does haunt us because it does create an image that everything is competing for space, food, territory and food. Of course it is easy to see this to be the case as at an outer level this is how life appears to go on. Things compete with other things, plants battle for space and animals eat each other and / or develop ever more sophisticated ways to prevent themselves being eaten.

This creates the classic image of a pyramid of power within nature with the strongest and most evolved (which is we humans) at the top of the pyramid. Because we are at the top of the pyramid we can exercise dominance and control over all that is below us in the chain. Or at least that is theory.

But in reality life is much more complicated and sophisticated than that. For nowhere in nature does any species only have a relationship with any one other species (be it plant or animal or both). And so the classic view of predator and prey is far too simplistic a view to be truly sustainable and accurate. Otherwise one would end up with the scenario that species wipe each other out to their ultimate own demise.

The matrix of relationships within nature suggest that life is much subtler than that and tends to indicate that

Wallace's view of natural selection is closer to the truth than that of Darwin. For predators do not chase and catch the strongest specimens of the prey species as a rule, but rather the weakest as they are the ones that are least likely to get away.

When males *"compete"* for the right to mate with females of the species in a test of strength and virility, it is not so much that the stronger male gets to mate and therefore pass on his genes to the next generation but rather than the weaker males don't and so their genes do not go forward. For all males have the possibility of mating if given the chance, but nature withdraws that chance from the less advantageous specimens and by this process of elimination the best genes go forward.

This has to be thought about most carefully because it is not some kind of a justification for the elimination of the weak and vulnerable but rather a natural selection of the best going forward for the benefit of the whole species. In this way undesirable or less favourable traits and characteristics can be de-selected or eradicated so that the species is left healthier, stronger and better adapted to meet the challenges. With this model of evolution refinement is the way forward.

With the Darwinian model of only the strong survive and the bottom line survival strategy is summated by the maxim – every man for himself. Which helps to explain why the perception that genes might be selfish has got in to the popular consciousness about how evolution works.

However, this selfish me first, me last and any more me again attitude is very unevolved behaviour and also very dangerous to the species itself. For within the Wallace model of natural selection there is a collaborative aspect to the process and how it works. For very rarely in nature where two males engage in a test of strength does one male kill the other. Usually what happens is that they work out which male is the stronger and he gets the territory and the other male accepts this result and moves away to try and find another territory or opportunity.

Killing the opponent is never the prime objective or motive.

In the Darwinian model it is, for the attitude is eat or be eaten, and this interpretation is quite prevalent in our modern day societies today with our empirical and hierarchical structures that dominate how life is lived and governed.

Within nature there is a subtler collaboration at play where the best of all species go forward in a process of refinement and adapting to meet new environments and new challenges.

Without a deeper feeling about how the whole fits together it is tempting to see the reasons for things as being purely physical, mechanistic and deterministic, whereas in truth that are much more integrated, holistic and subtle.

The more scientists probe the micro world looking for the reasons for things the more those reasons seem to become ever more elusive and esoteric.

The Hadron Collider is supposed to have been worth spending all that money on it because it may have proved that the Higgs Boson exists and the Higgs Boson apparently tells us why "stuff" exists.

No it doesn't.

It may tell us more about the process by which "stuff" condenses and appears but it doesn't tell us why it exists.

The reason that stuff appears is nowhere near the same thing as to **why** it appears.

The head looks for the facts.
The heart looks for the feeling.

That's why we say it is the heart that falls in love and not the head.

Perhaps now the Hadron Collider will turn its attention on love and put a human heart in there and send it round and round at near to the speed of light until they isolate all the separate bits until they find the Love Particle?

That is probably the last thing that they are likely to find.

The whole is, and always was, greater than the sum of the individual parts. We don't fall in love with a bunch or organs, nerves, bones and flesh we fall in love with a person.

Surely the sum of the various parts of the human race working together collectively and collaboratively towards a shared and refining future is better than a bunch of individuals competing for ever decreasing resources on a rapidly shrinking planet?

Darwinism is all about surviving.
Wallaceism is all about thriving.

Good on you Alfred, your time is upon us.

A good head and a good heart are always a formidable combination.

Nelson Mandela

Given that Nelson Mandela spent over 27 years in prison as a result of fighting for a cause he passionately believed in, which was equal rights and freedom for black South Africans, he has impeccable credentials for speaking about the relationship between the head and the heart.

Especially when one thinks about how he crystallised his life experience in such a way that he was able to lead his country to a new beginning in the post-apartheid era when he was elected to be its first president. And how he initiated, promoted and led the Truth and Reconciliation process that enabled profound and deep legacy issues to be better dealt with than they would have been had such a process not taken place.

It must have been hard for Mandela to maintain belief, hope and optimism whilst he was in prison, and no doubt he went through the dark night of the soul on many occasions during that time. Especially when one considers some of the horrible treatment he and the other prisoners were subjected to during that period.

Mandela was once asked that given the treatment that he was subjected to whilst he was prison did he ever come to hate any of the guards who mistreated and abused him. His answer was that he never would allow himself to hate them, because if he did that would show that they had won.

This certainly shows that he had developed a great awareness of himself and the nature of the struggle for freedom. For in seeking to escape what one is oppressed by in the search for freedom one has to be so careful not to make a prison for oneself by using the bricks and mortar of hate, bitterness, revenge and score settling. One has to remember that the struggle is to be free and *not* to eliminate that which caused the freedom to be withdrawn in the first place.

In order to do this a person has to find a clean, intact, sacred, natural space inside themselves that is free from the oppression of others and that of self because no bars can imprison the mind and the heart without our knowledge and consent.

Perhaps this is what Nelson Mandela speaks of when he says that the head and the heart when they work together can be a formidable team. For if the thinking is in sympathy with the feelings and the feelings are aligned with the thinking then they truly are a formidable team that combines the very best of both sides of our living experience.

It seems therefore that the head and the heart have four possible ways in which they do (or don't) work together and it is worth exploring these to see what the possible processes and outcomes might be.

So the four ways that the head and the heart can combine using Mandela's quote are as follows:

Head	Good
Heart	Good
Head	Good
Heart	Bad

Head	Bad
Heart	Good

Head	Bad
Heart	Bad

So to explore these possibilities let's begin by tackling the worst first.

Bad Head   Bad Heart

This obviously combines the worst of both worlds and is therefore a very dark space and place for a person to find themselves to be in. They don't think about things in a constructive or useful way and somehow they have also managed to suppress certain human feelings that enable them to act without compunction, compassion or humanity or any consideration for the feelings and need of others.

Such people become the centre of their own universe and they are able to rationalise their experience and what they do according to their own paradigm of what they regard as being important i.e. themselves. They are very good at compartmentalising things and separating out morality and standards from their conduct because their attitude is that end justifies the means and since they themselves are both the end and the means and as long as something benefits them then that is all that matters.

Other people aren't really seen as sentient beings and therefore their needs and feelings do not come into the equation at all. They are commodities which can be used and traded in for the person to obtain what they want. The same principle applies to everything from animals to possessions to the planet to resources to countries to money to relationships at every level.

Everything is fair game and everything is there for the taking.

This is Darwinism at it most raw, for it truly is a case of survival of the fittest. Feelings and sensitivities are for the weak as they only get in the way and dull the true sensitivities which are based in being at the top of the power pyramid at all costs. The guiding principle here is, do not mind who you have to climb over to get where you want to go or what you have to do to get there.

Conquer or be conquered is the mantra that is adopted with such people and world history is littered with examples of such tyrants and bullies who have besmirched and sullied the term human beings to make such a phrase totally alien to all they are and all they stand for and represent.

Ultimately however such people come unstuck and hoist themselves on their own petard, because at some point a tyrant is going to meet another tyrant who will out tyrant them.

Also in terms of longer term evolutionary processes such conduct isn't sustainable for it is ultimately self and species defeating. Nature regulates its processes in such a way that diversity is a cornerstone within how it operates and if anyone or anything thinks that it is bigger and better than such a system then they will soon enough find out that they are not.

In terms of human experience however it is an ongoing struggle for humans to escape this cycle of creating dominator structures and then breaking them down by way of revolution rather than evolution. Nature breaks things down in a natural and organic way and then recycles them for future use. But when the things that have been created aren't based on natural systems in the first place then there is an obvious problem to be addressed.

The natural systems being spoken of here are how to think and what to feel.

If this become more naturalised (both at the individual and collective level) then matters become clearer and an evolutionary as opposed to a revolutionary path forward is more likely to be found.

Bad Head   Good Heart

The first thing that could be said about this relationship is that it is full of contradiction and therefore so must be the person. For their head is telling them one thing and their heart is telling them something completely different and probably the complete opposite.

It wouldn't be at all surprising to find such people suffering from a headache about what to do a lot of the time. A sure fire sign of this happening is when you see people rubbing their neck when trying to decide what to do. For this is where the systems of the head and those of the heart meet in what should normally be something like a de-militarised zone. But because they are in conflict it literally gives the person a "pain in the neck". So they instinctively rub themselves in the neck to try and remove the tension and stress that has accumulated there.

When there is such a disconnection between two systems such as this then generally the lower system "wins" because it uses its power to bully the higher power, which always seeks to avoid conflict, into doing what it wants. This is unless the person listens to the higher system and instructs the lower system to follow the guidance of the higher system.

In this case the head usually ends up winning out over the heart. In such a scenario the person thinks and thinks and thinks about the problem, and also the possible permutations, and then tries to calculate which option to choose to get the desired result. But the problem with this approach is what the person thinks is important.

Because it is the head that is "bad" in this combination it tends to think in an unnatural and inefficient way which usually means thinking in a, me first me last and any more left over then me again kind, of a way. And when a person is bad in the head then the only thoughts available to them are ones that they already have in their head, and so it is very difficult for them to them in a new or original or integrated way about the situation or problem.

Thinking is linking, and so a person can end up going round and round in circles and prevaricating about the situation because their thinking is not cool, continuous and contained. Therefore, they end up getting dispersed and thereby compound the problem.

They keep getting stuck in wondering what to think and what to do rather than perhaps stopping and pausing and considering how they should think about the situation. If they do this, then this helps to stop the linking to bad thinking and makes the situation being faced less personal.

It would also help to listen to what their heart feels about the situation because in this combination the heart is "good" and therefore it can show the head the way forward through feelings and instincts.

For how many times have we got stuck in this combination of bad head, good heart and then listened to the head and made a decision that was completely wrong against what was needed and then reflected afterwards: *"I knew I should have listened to my instinct!"*

Probably as many as we have listened to the heart!

Good Head   Bad Heart

This combination is a very tricky one indeed and much rarer than the bad head good heart combination, particularly in our modern cultures where our education systems are bombarding us continuously in our brains about what and how we should think.

The evidence for this one being rarer is in things like saying that when someone has done something wrong but they mean well is that *"At least his or her heart is in the right place."* We don't say the converse when someone does something wrong due to a bad heart process that: *"Oh well at least his or her head was in the right place."*

Our modern cultures are very "brainy" and therefore the centre of gravity in our processes has shifted very much from the heart to the head. It is much more likely that the head will be swayed than rather than the heart. If one is in any doubt about this, then one just has to consider the fact of how our cities are designed and constructed with very little consideration given to arranging them around natural processes but rather grids and so called efficiency being the priorities.

Yet in reality they are more like gigantic prisons. Given that for the first time in human history there are now more people living in cities than there are on the land or in rural communities this is a worrying trend that causes many to forget or perhaps never truly experience what it is like to live on and with nature and the planet and what that feels like.

If the head is in balance and the heart is not, then this suggests that whilst a person has a moral code and a set of principles that they know are right, they nevertheless allow themselves to be governed by a lower set of feelings and emotions.

Such things as revenge, hatred, greed and lust are more powerful in the person and they simply cannot stop themselves from being governed by these appetites for that is what they surely are. The seven virtues lose out to the seven deadly sins every time when the heart out of balance rules the head.

Good Head   Good Heart

Eureka and at last we have it!

A fully functional, integrated, connected, throughout human being.

With a heart of gold and a head for heights!

We are clearly designed to both think and feel, and each has its own nature, process and function that stands on its own account and complements the other. Neither is meant to dominate the other, but rather together build a platform where we can both give and receive from the very best of ourselves.

This may seem like a remote and unattainable place for us to reach, but in reality it is not far away at all, but already within us to find and be. For the truth of ourselves cannot be anywhere other than where we already are. It simply needs us to be natural, and use the faculties that we have been gifted in the way they were designed to be used.

Granted, sometimes these faculties can be culturally conditioned into being used for lesser or even warped purposes. This is where we go astray and become removed from ourselves and thus cause damage to ourselves, others, the planet and possible the future.

The path back to being natural is not to ask oneself the question how to get things from their use but rather how they can best be used and for what purpose?

To think it is to create it, and to create it is to give something life and freedom.

Every thought and every feeling resonates to the further most edges of the Universe and across the ages through time and space. We are therefore what we think and feel and by connection so is the Universe. It matters, for what we think and feel changes the very substance of the Universe in small but real and powerful ways.

Have the thought that you would want to be thought. Feel the feeling that you would want to be felt.

Be moved by that which you would want things to be moved by.

Be the person you would want to see in the world.
For only you can be that person.

And if not now, then when?

Despite everything, I believe that people are really good at heart.

Anne Frank

As everyone probably knows, Anne Frank was a Jewish Dutch girl who died in the Second World War in a concentration camp (Bergen Belsen). She was largely just another statistic at the time, but she subsequently became world famous when her father Otto discovered and published her diary. The diary has been translated into literally dozens of languages and sold millions of copies since it was first published.

It is hauntingly beautiful, full of the ordinary ups and downs of a teenage girl growing up and coming to terms with her changes from being a girl towards a young woman. And yet this all occurs within the context of a moment by moment life and death struggle of hiding from an enemy who would, and eventually did, put them to death if and when they were found.

As a testament to Anne Frank's fame, when the name Anne is typed into a search engine it is her name that comes up first as the most commonly researched.

Anne was originally from Munich in Germany, but her family left Germany in 1933 when Anne was about 4 years old and moved to Amsterdam in Holland to live, as her mother and father felt it was no longer safe to live as Jews in Germany with the rise of the Nazi party into power.

The family then lived in Amsterdam up to and including the outbreak of the Second World War. They then found themselves unable to escape from Holland when the Nazis invaded and occupied the country, so they had to go in to hiding to try and avoid detection and probable transportation back to Germany to the concentration camps there.

The family went in to hiding on 6th July 1942 and were discovered and arrested on 4th August 1944. From there the family was transported back to the concentration camps in Germany (initially to Auschwitz). Then they were separated and Anne ended up in Bergen Belsen with her older sister Margot. They both died there within a few days of each other in March 1945, sadly not that long before the end of the war and less than a month before the camp was liberated by British forces on 15 April 1945.

It is not known exactly what the cause of Anne's death was but it was probably either Typhus, as the disease swept the concentration camp at the time killing up to 17,000 prisoners, or it may have been simply starvation.

Meanwhile her father Otto somehow survived his time in Auschwitz, and after the camp was liberated he was given his daughter's diary in July 1945 alongside some of her other humble possessions. He later stated that he had no idea that Anne had been keeping a diary during their time in hiding in Holland, and he was quite understandably deeply and profoundly moved by his daughter's private and intimate recording of her and her family's events, feelings and emotions during this period. It was also very painful for him to go through what was written as not only was he a part of those experiences, but it was his now dead daughter who was speaking to him again from beyond the grave about those experiences in ways that he never knew she felt at the time they were happening.

Otto began considering whether to publish the diary as he felt that others would benefit from reading about the experiences of a young girl growing up during these horrific experiences. He especially felt it would be useful given the beauty of Anne's writing and the message it carried for humanity. And despite the fact that Anne had herself said several times within her writing that the diary would never be seen by anyone else, he also considered her wish to one day be a published writer alongside the fact that the diary had a message for all.

He therefore decided on balance to have the diary published and despite initially being rejected it was duly published in Holland in 1947.

Since that time its message has spread far and wide across the world as a haunting reminder of the appalling consequences of war on the lives of ordinary people, the reality of man's hatred of man and what it will cause people to do. And all of this is mixed in with the thoughts, emotions and feelings of a young girl growing up inside the claustrophobic experience of hiding from the invaders of her country for fear of being discovered.

The diary was given to Anne by her father Otto as a present on her 13th birthday the 12th June 1942 and she immediately began writing in it on that date recording her thoughts, impressions and feelings. It was originally produced to be an autograph book but Anne decided to use it as a diary and its last entry is dated 1st August 1944 just before the Frank family were discovered in their hiding place and arrested.

The diary therefore covers a period of just over two years from soon after Anne turns 13 until she is 15 with all but the first month of that period being the time that the family were in hiding until just a couple of days before they were discovered.

In thinking about the times that Anne grew up and when she was writing her diary it is very hard to imagine what it must have been like to live with such fear and uncertainty in such terrible conditions never knowing what the next day, the next hour, the next minute might bring. Certainly to modern lives in the West living 70 years later (including that of the writer) it is hard if not impossible to imagine what it must have been like to be living in such a way as not being able to go out on the street without being arrested and transported to almost certain death simply for being born into a particular race or religion.

It is easy to forget that this was only 70 years ago in what many think is the civilised West and indeed it has continued into the modern era with just as potent attitudes of hatred and debasement, sanitised somewhat away from the truth of what they really are of genocide and holocaust via terms such as ethnic cleansing.

But as stated most modern people do not have experiences of such awful trauma in their lives where simply being alive is regarded by others as being a crime that warrants punishment by death.

Yet within this incredible set of hardships faced by Anne and her family she managed to write something that was full of light and hope and which has continued to be a source of inspiration for millions since it was first published.

Perhaps it needs such pressures and hardship for something truly to be born? For it is only when people are really stretched that they find out and reveal who and what they really are in their core. Much like the process of how a glittering diamond is formed inside the earth for it is the intense stresses and pressures that are placed on the carbon that "forces" it into becoming something truly dazzling.

If the pressure isn't that great, then it forms something different such as graphite. Perhaps if the pressures to be something better than the pressure upon us isn't that great then we can end up being or settling for lesser than who and what we really are?

Would we have ever heard of Anne Frank if the Second World War didn't occur and the Nazi policy of The Final Solution hadn't been embarked on? We shall never know, but what we do know is that those things did take place and we most certainly have heard of Anne Frank both tragically and thankfully.

In going back to the different forms of carbon and how they appear in solid form it is interesting that under the greatest pressures where carbon forms into diamonds, the form it takes is transparent and full of light whereas when the external pressures are lesser it becomes graphite and this is both dark and opaque.

Perhaps therefore it needs something greater than ourselves (whatever that need might be) to exert itself upon us in order for us to become what may be hidden from us whilst we ourselves seek lives of less stress and pressure and try and find lives that are as comfortable as possible?

This isn't saying that one should wear the hair shirt and avoid comfort at all cost, but it does suggest that the seeking of greater and greater comfortability can weaken the inner core of who we are and what can be.

For unless there is a need to discover something inside oneself that one might not know or believe is there then it may never be discovered. It certainly cannot be discovered in a theoretical or intellectual way. This is much like the story of the mother who when she saw that a car had rolled on to and had pinned her son under it, suddenly found the strength to lift the car off her son and hold it up until help arrived to remove her son from underneath.

This kind of action was and is impossible to the so called "normal" life. But in an exigency people can and do find incredible resources upon which to draw whether that be physically, emotionally or spiritually or indeed all three.

This then asks the question as to which life we regard as being "normal". Is the day to day ordinary life of habit and routine or is the life when we are stretched beyond our usual boundaries of existing and carrying on from day to day or is it the life where we step out of or are forced out of what we think we can do in to what we simply have to do or perhaps more rightly, cannot not do?

The place where the possible becomes improbable and the impossible becomes possible.

It is said that necessity is the mother of invention. That is a profound truth but it does ask the question – exactly what is the necessity that leads to the invention in the first place? For are all so called necessities that led to inventions truly "necessary"?

And perhaps also the saying has a secret twin which could read: *"Necessity is the father of discovery."*

For sometimes things may indeed need to be invented but perhaps on others they are already there but simply waiting to be discovered when the need arises.

Whatever the case it is clear that the timing of Anne Frank being given the diary by her father on her birthday such a short time before they were forced to go in to hiding was such that Anne and later the world were able to discover just what lived in her heart that we may never have known about had she not lived in such circumstances.

For without living inside such a reality the phrase *"Despite everything I believe that people are really good at heart"* couldn't have such poignancy and profundity.

Given their circumstances it would be easy to believe that those who pursued them seemed to have no good in their hearts. Yet Anne chose not to hold that view no matter what the evidence was to the contrary. In her heart she clearly decided not to make a home for hatred, prejudice, judgement, resentment and bitterness.

It is easy to say that she is just a naïve young girl full of fantasy and idealism when she is writing in her diary, but that would be to miss the point.

She decides to hold the best and recognises that the heart is where the truth of oneself and what one believes about others truly lies.

She holds the view that no matter what life does to us and how we may behave, perhaps sometimes in a cruel and uncaring way, that beneath it all naturally people have a good heart which generally chooses to hold the best about others whether or not they hold it about themselves.

This speaks of the higher case where being human is concerned. It is the lesser of ourselves that causes us not to be "good". So why be lesser when you can be more?

And what does it take for a person to find the more of themselves?

Finding a need that is bigger than them.

We all have a bit of Anne Frank living inside of us somewhere.

The proof is that we all have a heart.

All we have to do is open up our hearts and let the sun shine in.

Write it on your heart that every day is the best day in the year.

Ralph Waldo Emerson

The alternatives to each day not being the best day of the year are not really that attractive or promising and certainly do not carry any sense of hope or optimism.

Perhaps the worst case scenario is that the day didn't happen at all, and therefore not only would the day be neither the best nor worst in the year, but rather it doesn't exist and therefore probably neither do you. As such it wouldn't be possible to compare it to any other day of the year for not even God can compare something to something that doesn't exist. Nor would there be something or someone to compare the something to the nothing!

Although this would mean that there wouldn't be anything to complain or be unhappy about, it would also mean that conversely there wouldn't be anyone or anything to be happy about either. Welcome to limbo!

Even at the very first level of appreciating what Emerson has to say it is clear that he is definitely on to a winner, for each day that a person has is far, far better than the one that they didn't have. And yes some days, where things appear to go really well, are on the face of it apparently far better than others where things are hard and a struggle, the ultimate option of having no day at all in which to struggle or find it hard because the day doesn't exist isn't that great a choice.

Since the Earth came into existence approximately 4.66 billion years ago, (despite some claims that the Earth was in fact created by God on 23rd October 4004 BC at 9am) there have been about 1,979,000,000,000 or nearly 2 trillion days since that time. And since we may each have on average four score and ten years of life whilst we are here (which is 25,550 days) that represents a percentage of the time of the life of the Earth of something in the order of 0.0000152%.

It's not that long really is it?

Or in thinking about it in another way, if the whole of the Earth's history was compressed into a single calendar year then the human race, which effectively emerged approximately 3 million years ago, would only appear in that calendar year at 3 minutes to midnight on the 31st December and a person who is 70 years old today would only have been born at ¾ of a second before midnight on that last day.

This would mean that a single day such as today would only occupy 0.0000293 of a second in such an Earth year.

No wonder the days seem to fly by at times!

Still, it could be even worse for the Earth is only 4.6 billion years old whereas the Universe is approximately 13.8 billion years old and so if the comparison was made to the life of the Universe then the days would seem to be 2/3 shorter still!

Surely this brings new light to the expression to make the most of each and every day you have, for not only can you not have them twice, but also in the light of the life of the Earth and the Universe they truly pass in the twinkle of an eye. In fact, far less than that in relative terms because the blink of an eye is positively snail like when compared the passing of time in Universal terms.

Yet although each day is but a tiny moment in the life of the cosmos without each and every moment contributing to the great mosaic of life itself what would there be to savour, be thankful for and even experience? And without us experiencing each and every moment that life causes us to be in process of, what would the Universe not be experiencing of itself?

Indeed, what would we ourselves be if weren't part of the theatre of its happening as co-writers and co-creators of its story and play?

No wonder Shakespeare said:

"All the world's a stage,
And all the men and women merely players;
They have their exits and their entrances,
And one man in his time plays many parts."

For parts we surely are of the greater whole.

Like every play it needs for each and every part (however large or small) to work for the whole to function to its best possibility.

As it is above so it is below, for if each part of the Universe does not work to its best capacity and potential then somehow the whole suffers as a result. The opposite is also true for if each and every part works to its optimum then that very fact helps all of the other parts work to their maximum possibility too.

Just as every cell in the human body is unique and different and is part of perhaps a more specific function such as the brain or a kidney or a bone or the skin or indeed the heart itself, without each individual cell working the whole suffers to a tiny but real degree.

If every moment isn't the best moment it can be in that particular place within the space time continuum, then somehow the whole space continuum is lesser for that fact as is the particular life that that lesser moment is happening to.

This also suggests that it is a very wise maxim that states – never put off until tomorrow what you can do today.

Perhaps this is true for a number of reasons.

Firstly, it is impossible to put off until tomorrow what you might have done today because the moment in which one tries to do it tomorrow will be a completely different one, especially as the moment that might have existed tomorrow will have changed irrevocably by the fact that what wasn't done yesterday wasn't done. The domino effect of that default is that each and every moment that has occurred since the original default of not doing yesterday what could have been done then has been altered forever more.

This means that if and when the thing that was going to be done yesterday is attempted to be done today then it isn't and cannot be the same thing any more because the thing itself and everything else that it is related to has been changed by the non doing yesterday and so also has the person attempting the doing changed because they too are affected by what they didn't do yesterday!

So it's not the same person attempting to do the thing that wasn't done and what they are now attempting to do isn't the same thing either!

Secondly, it is also important not to put things off until tomorrow when perhaps one thinks one has more time, because as seen above in relative terms time passes before one has a chance to blink. Tomorrow, if indeed it ever comes, slips by just as fast as the relative microsecond that today is and yesterday becomes tomorrow just as fast if not faster than tomorrow becomes yesterday.

This can lead to a person questioning the maxim – there is no time like the present – because they are so busy putting things off until tomorrow that somehow they don't ever feel that there is any time to do anything. Not only is there no time to do anything, but they themselves in a way are not present for they are attempting to occupy some hypothetical moment in the future (that may or may not come into existence) and so as a thing cannot occupy two different moments and places at the same time they cannot therefore be in the present moment. Which is a shame, because the present moment is the only one that they can truly occupy and influence and also function properly in.

It is also unnatural and perverse against the true nature of things for the heart doesn't put off beating until tomorrow because it can't be bothered doing it today. It does the very best beating it can in every moment we experience life, whether that be at rest, work or during vigorous exercise. It tries to work at maximum capacity in response to the need of the whole that it serves so that the whole can function at optimum to serve that need.

This is surely a great lesson to be learned by us all.

It makes the whole seem like a giant, inter-connected and an integrated network which of course it is. As it is said – a chain is only as strong as its weakest link. Perhaps a life is only as strong as its weakest moment? Or more probably the moment that hasn't been experienced or put off until another day.

It is interesting that if someone hasn't given of their best in any given circumstance we often say that their heart wasn't in it. If this was literally true, then it would of course have disastrous consequences for the person. But perhaps the same applies in the figurative sense as well. For if a person's heart isn't in what they do then in a way what this is saying is that they themselves aren't in it either. They are not present and if they are not present then by the law of displacement they must be absent.

Absent from what? Themselves and the moment, and therefore from the flow of life itself.

What Emerson seems to be speaking of is having a mindfulness and a presence of mind in order that we do not become complacent, blasé or familiar. Also the importance of having a thankfulness and gratitude for the gift of life itself.

For as the ancients knew, to think it is to create it.

If we therefore think the glass is half empty, then that is what it is. If we think that it is half full then that too is what it is. But if we are thirsty for its contents then we are simply delighted and grateful that there is something in the world that can satiate our vital need for water in order that we can enjoy the next moment.

Imagine what kind of world it would be if everyone in it was simply grateful for the fact that they could experience the fullness of the next moment. And imagine what it would be like if every person on Earth lived their life as though every day was the best day of the year.

Consider just what kind of a difference this would make to today, tomorrow, next year and into the future and beyond.

There is the saying that today is the first day of the rest of your life. That statement is clearly true for none of us know just how many days we may have left alive.

But imagine what it would be like if we all only had one day left and that it was this day.

Imagine how heightened our experiences would be on that day.

How sacred and special it would be for us all.

Well who is to say that it can't be like that anyway? For whatever happens in the future, today always **is** the only day we have left.

Your heart knows this to be true even if you don't. Otherwise it might ask for a day "off".

We can learn a lot from our loyal, faithful and true allies and servants that love us and keep us alive. For they hold the best of us even if at times we don't hold the best of ourselves.

There is something safe and reassuring about the way that things work. Things may not be perfect but they do their best.

In the light of so many things doing their best all around us and even in us it seems churlish not to try and respond in kind.

So how does one do one's best on any given day? That's easy.

Do your best to do your best.
And leave the rest to the better rest! ☺

A man finds himself, to his great astonishment, suddenly existing, after thousands of years of non-existence; he lives for a little while; and then, again, comes an equally long period when he must exist no more. The heart rebels against this, and feels that it cannot be true.

Arthur Schopenhauer.

The word astonishment has more than one meaning in common usage today. It can mean either total surprise on the one hand or that something is absolutely amazing beyond belief almost on the other.

Perhaps both meanings apply in equal measure to the fact that each and every one of us, like the man in the above quote, find ourselves to be suddenly existing. No wonder we all pretty much without exception, cry when we arrive via the magical and mystical experience of being born.

For whatever way one looks at it, the process of being born and coming into existence in carnal human form is truly extraordinary. The odds against each and every one of us ever coming into existence in the first place are absolutely huge. Yet each person who reads this, and of course all those who don't, must have by a series (and a very long series at that) of fortunate circumstances, defied the odds and obstacles and made it from being nothing to something. And a very specific something at that i.e. themselves.

The quote from Schopenhauer is very haunting for it resonates with us at one level in that we all feel that there is point before which we tend to think that we didn't exist. For many that would be a point before the moment of conception. There is obviously a much debated issue as to when life as a human being actually commences, with some saying that it is at the very moment of conception and others saying that it is much later when the foetus starts to become viable as a separate human life.

Yet very few people would suggest that a person exists before the fact of conception or in other words, leaving aside the possibility of artificial insemination for a moment, that a person exists before the act of sexual intercourse between their parents which led to the egg of their mother being fertilised by the sperm of their father.

Or if they did then you would end up with the rather bizarre scenario of asserting that a person "exists" before their parents did and before their grandparents had the acts of intercourse that lead to their parents being conceived and the acts of intercourse that led to their grandparents being conceived to all the way back to when Adam and Eve (however and whenever they were conceived) and beyond even that!

Yet is that notion as totally bizarre as it possibly seems at first instance?

For this asks deep and profound philosophical questions like what do we mean by concepts such as something, nothing and existence? And following on from that an even deeper question which is, why do we and things generally exist at all? In other words, why is there something rather than nothing and why and how therefore did we move from being part of the nothing to becoming part of the something and what happens to us when we cease to be part of the something?

Do we revert back to being part of the nothing and if so is that part of the same nothing that we were part of before we appeared in the something or is it a different kind of nothing occupying a different piece of time and space to the previous nothing we were part of or is it a new one? If it is a new kind of nothing just how many types of nothing are there and what are they made of, smaller bits of nothing?

In case this philosophical line of reasoning seems far fetched and ridiculous, the same difficulty in deciding what something is or isn't faces science in the physical realm as well. For whilst we know what a human being is and looks like, what happens when you take a leg away? Or both legs, or all four limbs, or the head? And what if you keep cutting a person up into smaller and smaller bits until you get down to subatomic level? Eventually when you get past what is or isn't the Higgs Boson and cut again the person and the stuff they appear to be made of disappears into the ether, perhaps to where they came from in the first place?

Or on the other hand if you take just one cell off a living person can you that that is "them"?

Everyone would say that one cell isn't the person. But just how many cells does it take to make the person "them"? One hundred? A thousand? A million? A billion? A trillion?

Not only that but how do those cells (however many it takes to make a human being) need to be arranged into a specific shape to such a point that it can be safely said that that particularly arrangement is in fact a human being? Plus, who or what does the arranging in the first place. And who or what arranges the arranger?

Phew!

No wonder it is hard at times to know just who and what one is, where has come from and where one might be going next!

This state of affairs can easily lead to a contradiction between the head and the heart that Schopenhauer speaks of.

For whilst the head might comprehend and understand that existence is a carnal reality whilst we occupy human form and that outside of that particular state we don't exist, the heart cannot accept that existence is so black and white and that outside of the short time we spend here there is nothing but a meaningless void.

In other words, if we just rely on what the logic of the brain tells us then that leads to the world and our own existence being nothing more, or less, than meaningless. A case of – now you see me and now you don't or more precisely – first you don't see me, now you do and now you don't again.

A terrible case of reverse magic of the worst kind. Instead of the magician pulling a rabbit out of the hat it is a case of the magician causing a human being to firstly to appear out of nothing, but then in a nasty twist to the trick they allow them to exist for a short time and then cause them to disappear back into nothingness again, forever.

No wonder the heart rebels at this thought.

Are we doomed to think of ourselves as nothing more than an arbitrary and meaningless mix of chemistry, biology, physics and astronomy? A sophisticated cosmic soup of chance and luck that just happens to exist, but could just as easily not exist?

But what of art and poetry and music of beauty and love? And yes even religion too? Are these too simply quirky side effects of the business of being alive? Are they to be explained away by the fact that there is some evolutionary advantage to them appearing rather than not appearing?

Is the music of Beethoven and Mozart nothing more than noise that helps us continue rather than not continue?

Are the poetry and writings of Plato, Dante, Shakespeare, Dickens and Jane Austen simply nothing more than clever DNA sequencing that do nothing more than ensure that our species has the best possible chance of survival?

Is the painting and sculpture of Titian, Rembrandt, Leonardo d Vinci and Vincent van Gogh not really art and beautiful of its own account, but rather somehow a clever trick by nature to make us like it so that we ensure future generations like it too and thus ensure our continuance because there is something to like and therefore something to live for?

And what of love?

Is this too a trick of the mind or our selfish genes deluding us into thinking that we genuinely feel these feelings for another, whereas in reality they are nothing more than some clever chemicals ensuring we make choices strictly according to natural selection?

Are those profound feels of love and bonding that a mother feels for her new born baby simply nature's way of ensuring that the child has a best chance possible to discover whether it too in turn may be able to find out whether it can be naturally selected to pass on its genetic code to the next generation? Is that it?

Is the point of existence then merely to exist?
And to exist so that a naturally selected genetic package of oneself can be passed on to future generations so that they too can exist for no other rhyme or reason other than they too existed so that they could pass on their meaningless existence to future generations?

It is little wonder then that the heart rebels at the thought of such a cold and heartless universe!

Is it not true that great art, music, theatre, philosophy and even religion help soften and warm what might otherwise be a cold, dark and meaningless existence? They may offer no more than that, but even if that is all that they do offer then we should be grateful to them and for them in making this pointless existence more bearable!

Yet something says that they offer much more than that. This something speaks to and from the heart not the head. For some things can only be felt and understood through feelings rather than rationalisation, logic and deductive reasoning.

Otherwise the Mona Lisa is nothing more than different coloured paints slapped on to a blank bit of canvas and then stuck in a frame and hung in a gallery for no real purpose at all and certainly to no effect.

For a rhinoceros the Mona Lisa may well represent no more than that. But human beings are not rhinoceroses in all their senses and sensibilities.

We have evolved differently and developed different senses and sensibilities and these must exist for a reason.

If we have evolved the ability to feel love, hope, joy, compassion, care, humanity, kindness, empathy, awe and wonder then these must exist for a purpose and function.

Could it be because something that gave us the capacity to feel these things wanted us to feel them so that it could feel them too through our agency?

Well yes it **could** be for that reason because it is impossible to prove that it wasn't for that reason! Although it has to be admitted that doesn't prove that it was for that reason either.

Some things cannot be proven to the ultimate satisfaction of the head.

It is impossible to prove that one is in love or whether it is just one's genes making mechanistic choices and selections to ensure their best chance of continuance and that the term "love" is just a smokescreen for what is nothing more than a series of sequential biological and chemical processes.

One can't prove that one is in love beyond the doubt of the uncertainty principle that says that one might not be. All one knows is that one **is** in love and that it feels great!

For the heart that might be just enough.

If someone ever thinks they have found some love in a test-tube or molecular formula, then it's highly likely that they have in fact found something else and it could be something not like love at all, but rather something rather icky!

Some things exist for a mere instant in time, serve their purpose and then move on. Other things are immortal and cannot be destroyed but change their form and evolve over time.

Who is to say that we ourselves as human beings are not made up of a combination of these flashing sequins and immortal and indelible sequences?

The head might doubt whether it is true.
But the heart might just know that it **is** true.

The answer might just depend on which bits of you you trust the most.

We do exist.

We have made our entrance and all the world's a play whilst we are here.

Exist = Exits.

Therefore, be careful which one you choose and why.

The only business of the head in the world is to bow a ceaseless obeisance to the heart.

William Butler Yeats

W.B. Yeats was an Irish poet whose life straddled the 19th and 20th centuries. His life witnessed the profound and radical changes that these "modernising" times brought to our world, and so he could see the shift from a more rural based way of living to an ever increasing movement towards greater and greater mechanisation and industrialisation, with more and more people moving from the countryside to live in cities to obtain work and live in cramped and overcrowded conditions.

Coupled with this, Yeats could see that alongside this physical shift there was a cultural, psychological, physiological and spiritual shift with matters of the heart becoming increasingly dominated by the analytical, logical and reductionist processes of the head, which saw things as things and results as goals, and with profits not prophets as being those things we should listen to most, loudest and longest.

Yeats himself was intensely interested in the human imagination and the power of the mind, and he was also fascinated by the esoteric and the occult in its many forms and how it expressed itself, not just through human beings but also through nature.

He found much solace in nature, and particularly loved to spend time in his beloved Sligo in the wilds of nature under the slopes of the moody Ben Bulben where he wrote much of his most famous work including The Lake Isle of Innisfree.

If one should travel to Inishfree even today one will find that it remains a special place with much of what Yeats saw and felt still present in special places and special moments behind the modern veil of ("Been there, done that, ticked it off").

I will arise and go now, and go to Innisfree,
And a small cabin build there, of clay and wattles
* made;*
Nine bean-rows will I have there, a hive for the
* honey-bee,*
And live alone in the bee-loud glade.

And I shall have some peace there, for peace comes
* dropping slow,*
Dropping from the veils of the morning to where the
* cricket sings;*
There midnight's all a glimmer, and noon a purple
* glow,*
And evening full of the linnet's wings.

I will arise and go now, for always night and day
I hear lake water lapping with low sounds by the
* shore;*
While I stand on the roadway, or on the pavements
* grey,*
I hear it in the deep heart's core.

There is so much more to this poem than just the words.

For what Mendelsohn said about music being what happens between the notes is just as true for poetry in that the real resonance lies between the words and not within the words themselves.

Otherwise how could the words *"I love you."* ever mean anything to anyone?

We know the resonance of things sometimes much more than we know the meaning of the words themselves.

It is a profound final line when Yeats writes - *"I hear it in the deep heart's core"*.

Mostly we hear things with our ears, and then those micro signals are transferred to the brain which in turn interprets both the meaning of the words that have been heard and also the response that should be given to them.

But what if instead of listening with our ears to what is being said or at an even deeper level what is being felt, we in fact listened with our hearts?

Is this in fact possible to do?
What does it cause and what does it allow?
What does it connect us to both inside and outside of ourselves?

We often hear ourselves and others say to each other when surrounded by a cacophony of unnatural noises especially in cities that we can't hear ourselves think.

Perhaps it is even worse in that being surrounded by and bombarded by such a plethora of alien and disorientating and dispersing and distracting invasive noises we can in fact no longer hear ourselves feel?

As TS Eliot, another poet whose life largely overlapped that of Yeats, put it:

> *Descend lower, descend only*
> *Into the world oJ perpetual solitude*
> *World not world, but that which is not world*
> *Internal darkness, deprivation*
> *And destitution oJ all property*
> *Desiccation oJ the world oJ sense*
> *Evacuation oJ the world oJ fancy*
> *Inoperancy oJ the world oJ spirit*
> *This is the one way, and the other*
> *Is the same, not in movement*
> *But abstention from movement; while the world moves*
> *In appetency on its metalled ways*
> *OJ time past and future.*

Within Eliot's bleak landscape of what our outer reality looks like when matters are of the heart and spirit are bulldozed and Tarmacadammed lies the denial of purpose, beauty and wonder where meaning is rendered meaningless and the meaningless is given meaning and even worshipped.

Or since we are quoting writers and musicians perhaps it was best summated by Joni Mitchell in her era defining song Big Yellow Taxi when she wrote:

> *Don't it always seem to go*
> *That you don't know what you get til it's gone*
> *They paved Paradise*
> *And put up a parking lot.*

The song doesn't say just exactly what the parking lot was built for, but perhaps it was for the tree museum or maybe for a nearby church so that the congregation can get there easily and so that the members can go and worship the God of Creation and all Nature?

Or maybe it's simply for the nearby shopping mall where they can spend their manna from heaven – money?

But in truth what meaning does money have unless it is believed in?
What purpose does it serve unless a purpose is invented for it? Which it was.
What can it really buy unless someone says it can, and others then believe that reason?

Can one really go out in to the great Church we call Nature and "buy" a carrot, a banana, a potato or a glass of water from a crystal clear spring?

All the money in the world cannot pull a carrot from the soil, pick a bunch of bananas from a tree or scoop a deliciously refreshing handful of clear, clean water from a spring.

The rationalists will often say that belief in some higher order, deity or intelligence is illogical, irrational and based in ignorance and superstition. But is the belief in things such as money being able to buy and "own" things any better?

Recently in England it was reported that a mountain was being sold. Does the mountain know that this is happening and that it is being sold into the ownership and therefore servitude of a human being?

Will it be aware that after millions of years of simply standing there and "being" that now it belongs to someone?

Much of Yeats's research into the esoteric was carried out within a movement known as The Golden Dawn and some of his beliefs are expressed in his work The Vision.

The Golden Dawn was very much a product of the Victorian era and the search for meaning through such things as spiritualism, metaphysics, theosophy, Masonic law and practice, Rosicrucianism, the Hermetic Kabbalah and transcendentalism.

It saw its origins in the "lost" knowledge of the ancients and believed powerfully in forces and powers beyond the material plane within the occult and esoteric worlds. It drew its inspiration and guidance inside such things as natural magic, alchemy and the secret and hidden arts of the initiate going back in time to such things as the emerald tablets of Hermes Trismegustus from which it saw its pedigree and truth to have originated.

Hermes Trismegustus received his name which means *"thrice great"* it is said because he knew the three parts of the wisdom of the whole universe which are alchemy, astrology, and theurgy (the study and practice of rites and rituals and particularly those to do with spiritual magic and the hidden power of natural forces).

The Golden Dawn sought access to these cause worlds, the places from which all things originate and from where all things derive both their mandate and their power source.

As Yeats says in The Vision: *"There can be neither cause nor effect when all things are co-eternal."*

As to his motives within the movement he has this to say:

"Some were looking for spiritual happiness or for some form of unknown power, but I had a practical object. I wished for a system of thought that would leave my imagination free to create as it chose and yet make all that it created, or could create, part of the one history, and that the soul's."

Yeats was seeking a bridge for and from the imagination into the unknown. Not a bridge that was made with concrete and steel and not one that was conjured up by the machinations of the brain, but one that was created from the opening of the heart to our true inner nature within and the harmony of the spheres from beyond.

In his view the opening of these doors could only be done by the opening of the heart which is why he speaks of the need of the head to be in obeisance to the heart. The yang needs to be led by the yin, the left hemisphere of the brain needs to be led by the right hemisphere, the masculine needs to follow the feminine.

Our reality is better understood through imagination, beauty and the wonders of nature and our appreciation of these things rather than us seeking to define our reality through analysis, logic and materialism.

We cannot reach for ourselves and the future, but we can arrange ourselves in a better and more effective way to receive it.

Who is there to say that Yeats was wrong?

Not anyone who has ever been in love or deeply moved by life, its beauty and its enigma it is supposed.

I love those who can smile in trouble, who can gather strength from distress, and grow brave by reflection. 'Tis the business of little minds to shrink, but they whose heart is firm, and whose conscience approves their conduct, will pursue their principles unto death.

Leonardo da Vinci

There is probably hardly a person, at least in the Western world anyway, who hasn't heard of Leonardo da Vinci. He was most certainly one of the most profoundly talented and influential geniuses who has ever lived. Artist, sculptor, scientist, philosopher, thinker, designer, architect, inventor, anatomist, researcher, mystic and man of mystery and so much more, he profoundly influenced almost every sphere of endeavour he turned his mind and faculty to. His influence is still deeply felt today.

Millions still flock to see his painting of the Mona Lisa in the Louvre each year and people are fascinated by his drawings and scientific researches that appear in many ways to be centuries ahead of their time. Every so often there seems to be a programme on TV that tries to turn one of Leonardo's drawings in to a flying machine that might actually fly.

He clearly captured and encapsulated the spirit of the Renaissance in so many ways with his passionate desire to know how and why things worked the way that they do, from nature herself to the nature of man. His penetrating and enquiring mind burned with desire to know the truth and how the truth worked and how it could best be expressed through human life, from how it conducted itself, to knowing its very essence and nature, through to its various forms of expression from art to sculpture to music to architecture to science and discovery and inventions that flowed there from.

The word prolific seems somehow to do his life a total disservice because it seems impossible for one life to have crammed so much in to it. Maybe we need another word like Leonardo to describe people who are prolific beyond the point of prolific?

Mind you, whilst Leonardo was extremely good at starting things but he wasn't always the best at getting things like commissions finished as his mind and interest would flit from one field of fascination to another as his fancy took him. Perhaps the fact that he was an Aries might go some way towards explaining why he so good at starting so many things but not so good at finishing them? ☺

But who else better represents the synergy and connection between science and art than Leonardo? The rational and the rapture, the freedom and the form, the technical and the imagined, the known and the unknowable, the physical and the spiritual, the seen and the unseen, the secular and the religious.

In many ways, what we know of Leonardo's life shows that it was a life of contradictions. But then that being the case who better to represent an example of the human condition, for are not all lives filled to one degree or another with contradictions? Do all lives not suffer both the pains and pleasures of living, the agony and the ecstasy, the sublime and the subjugated?

Perhaps the spirit of this contradiction is represented well in one of the verses from the Rubyiat of Omar Khyiam which reads:

I sent myself through the invisible,
Some letter of that After-life to spell:
And after many days my soul return'd
And said, "Behold, Myself am Heav'n and Hell".

We all embody something of this contradiction of being part heaven and part hell, for we all have the capacity to do good or evil, be carriers and generators of the light or agency for things that are dark and negate all that is fine.

We all feel that we fit in and belong at times and at other times we feel like aliens in an alien and hostile world.

We are all to one degree or another square pegs in a round hole, misfits trying to fit in.

Which is all rather fitting because one of Leonardo's most famous drawings is titled Vitruvian Man which was painted some time around 1490.

This is a stunning drawing because within the drawing Leonardo addresses the age old conundrum of whether or not it is possible to square the circle and of course circle the square!

The drawing illustrates Leonardo's deep understanding of science, art, nature and anatomy and fuses them all together in a brilliant marriage between the nature of man expressed through art and the art of nature as expressed through man.

One can therefore approach this drawing as a scientist or an art lover and not fail to be impressed by the synthesis that Leonardo's profound understanding and skill has brought to the subject and captured the interaction between the two in a simple yet deeply profound drawing of the human form as both a wonder of science and wonder of nature.

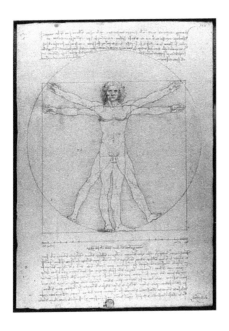

One can analyse the drawing and its proportions and the scientific principles contained within it for hours or equally one can simply gaze at it in a semi meditative state and be moved by its sheer poetic beauty.

In this one drawing Leonard seeks to capture and embody the principle of – to understand man one must study the Universe, to understand man one must study the Universe. Or expressed another way – as above so below.

Of course he succeeds brilliantly. He even manages to give some explanation of the drawing in some of his famous mirror writing which has to be read upside down in a mirror to make sense!

The drawing is sometimes called the Canon of Proportions because captured within it are relationships such as:

The length of the outspread arms is equal to the height of a man.
From the hairline to the bottom of the chin is one-tenth of the height of a man.
From below the chin to the top of the head is one-eighth of the height of a man.
From above the chest to the top of the head is one-sixth of the height of a man.
From above the chest to the hairline is one-seventh of the height of a man.
The maximum width of the shoulders is a quarter of the height of a man.
From the breasts to the top of the head is a quarter of the height of a man.
The distance from the elbow to the tip of the hand is a quarter of the height of a man.

And many more.

Somehow the science and the art of the picture melt all the so called differences between them and they merge into a representation of the human form that transcends time and space through the media of awe and wonder. It invites us to ask the question – just what does it mean to be human?

Who or what is the author of just such a design?
What does it represent?
What is it for?
What can it be and do?

It is a magnificent drawing, but such a brilliant mind and faculty as Leonardo's resists the compartmentalising of the human form into simply being this or that for surely the total is greater than the mere sum of the parts?

Perhaps this is something of what Leonardo means when he says: *"Tis the business of little minds to shrink."* For when we reduce things down to being smaller than they really are then we fail to see their true beauty, their real essence, their inner nature, their deeper truth.

In simple, the more we define things then the more we de-fine them in that we remove the fineness from them by seeing them as merely things. We cannot find the essence of why things are what they are by cutting them up and examining them under a microscope. A single kidney cell doesn't constitute what it means to be a human being, nor does the sum of all the cells that make up a human being do so either.

There is much magic, wonder and awe about how and why the whole comes together in an animated and vitalising way that in truth no one can explain because it comes from a realm that is beyond knowing in ways that our finite systems like to know things.

It is these finite systems that cause us to make things lesser than they truly are if we let these finite systems dominate our reality.

It is the infinite systems of ourselves such as art, joy, love, wonder, hope and belief that connect us to the truth of ourselves and our experience.

It is these parts of ourselves that enable us to accept and embrace what Leonardo expresses when he says:

"I love those who can smile in trouble, who can gather strength from distress, and grow brave by reflection."

Somehow within the struggle to be as one was meant to be, to live as one was meant to live, and to be as one was meant to be there is an endurance that endures even ourselves. For it connects us to the pedigree of what it means to be true to thine own self and all that that might mean.

Perhaps this lays the context for what Leonardo then goes on to say which is:

"They whose heart is firm, and whose conscience approves their conduct, will pursue their principles unto death."

For what is more important in life than having principles and living up to them? Better to die for a principle than to live for a lie.

At least that is what Leonardo clearly did in his own life despite the struggles, the resistances, the judgements that came his way.

A person's life here on this planet may be finite and mortal but the principle or principles that they live for need not be. And if a person dedicates their life to this principle then who is to say that they too thereby don't become immortal too?

In the words of the Welsh poet Dylan Thomas:

> *"Though lovers be lost, love shall not*
> *And death shall have no dominion."*

Leonardo clearly lives in on in many ways today nearly 500 years after his physical death and is clearly destined to do so for many more years to come.

For is death in fact a door not a wall, and are our heart, conscience and principles a set of keys that turn what looked like a brick wall into a door into another life, another Universe, another future?

You may not be another Leonardo.
That's OK we've already had one of those.

What we haven't had yet is another you or me.

At least until now that is!

Love is space and time measured by the heart.

Marcel Proust

What an amazing quote from a truly amazing man and writer!

There is something wonderful and awe inspiring in the words that begs the reader to abide with it, contemplate it, feel its richness and know that somehow, some way there is another world within, alongside and hidden from the known, the obvious and the strictly physical.

There are things in the Universe that can't be measured with a slide-rule, trigonometry, telescopes or arithmetic equations.

The proof of this truth lies in the fact that none of these *"instruments of the head"* have ever managed to find or locate the proof or otherwise of the existence of that ever elusive thing called love.

Yet we all know and feel it and sometimes in a way that floods every cell and fibre of our being.

Perhaps the world of space time continuum, as brought to us by Einstein, without the heart being involved simply reduces itself down to being the Universe as space and time alone? A mechanistic series of plotted points on a graph of vertical and horizontal grid that coldly and somewhat brutally says to the observer: "You are here."

But how did I get here?
And why?

And for what purpose?

How can I measure those things and with what can I measure them?

Can I find them in the Universe anywhere? Can I find them in myself?

Well as Proust seems to be suggesting one can't find them simply by using the tools of the head such as electron microscopes and telescopes alone.

A fixed, staring gaze at another person hardly encourages them to fall in love with you. It might in fact cause them to call the police instead!

But giving a person time and space to be who and what they really are, and to accept them for being just that truly is an act of love and kindness.

We have plenty of machines that try to measure time and space and in the 21st century we have some very sophisticated machines indeed to carry out this task.

But are any of them any more accurate than the heart in measuring what really matters about time and space?

For without the heart the measurement of time and space can only ever be about measuring "stuff" and the gaps in between it. But the heart measures not the gaps themselves but what lives within those gaps.

For unless things like love, hope, kindness and compassion live in the spaces between us then life is cold, lonely and empty.

To love and be loved is the true measurement of who and what we are and all that we can be. Because when we love and we are loved we find within ourselves the joy that we are blessed and gifted by not just those that love us or that we love, but by all that loves us and all that we love.

Love changes the time and space between things and shows that our linear measurements of time and space are in fact distortions of the true reality.

Just try being away from those you love and see what that does to your perception of time.

And do we not say that absence makes the heart grow fonder? So distance changes the reality and the feelings as well.

Proust knew that the heart was key in understanding what the head can never feel.

Falling in love, as Dr Spock might say, is illogical. It simply doesn't make any reasonable or rational sense and it doesn't seem to carry any obvious or immediate evolutionary advantage.

Of course it is illogical, that is why it is so fantastic!

And perhaps it does carry great evolutionary advantage because people who are in love with love, nature, other people, the future, whatever, tend to be healthier, happier and lead far more fulfilling lives than those who aren't.

So put down that microscope and slide rule for a moment and feel the moment of time and space that you, and you alone, now occupy. How amazing is that feeling that of all the other things that could have occupied that space and that particular moment that it is in fact only you that does?

So now that you have that moment and that space, what will you do with it?

The moment you have in your heart this extraordinary thing called love and feel the depth, the delight, the ecstasy of it, you will discover that for you the world is transformed.

Jiddu Krishnamurti

When I was a young man first arriving in London in the very early 1980's in a city with a population of three times the population of the whole of New Zealand I found myself in a completely different world to that which I grew up in.

Yes, it was what we called in New Zealand *"The mother country"*, even though all my ancestors were Irish, and yes the language was the same and many of the customs and traditions were the same or similar, but London was such a cosmopolitan place with so many diverse cultures and influences present, it was literally a world away from the one I grew up in.

And whilst New Zealand was a wonderful country to grow up in; safe, clean, beautiful and happy I soon began to realise on my travels that I had grown up within a narrow range of influences compared to the incredible diversity that existed elsewhere on the planet. So I resolved to explore some of these influences and beliefs when I got to London.

One of the first things I did when I arrived was to stay with my sister in Ealing, West London who had left New Zealand a couple of years before me and was now living in a squat (an empty house that the squatters had taken over of which there were many at the time) with a very cosmopolitan, diverse and interesting group of people!

After staying with her briefly I then ended up in my own squat with an equally interesting and diverse bunch people that had up to 9 different nationalities living it from diverse ethnic, cultural, social, religious, philosophical, moral and other points of views backgrounds. It was never boring that is for sure!

I even started my law career whilst living in this squat and each morning I would do a kind of reverse Superman by changing out of my Super-Squatter outfit and into my Super-Lawyer suit and tie and go out and save the world from nasty commercial contracts and things of such like.

In the evening I would come back home to the squat and change back into my Super-Squatter outfit and then revert to this person who was trying to find out who he really was outside the known of what he thought he was or what the world might decide he was if he didn't decide for himself.

To this end in my life as Super-Squatter I began to explore much of what London had to offer in terms of its alternative scene. There was always so much happening with different groups and movements be they, political, musical, social, philosophical, New Age and so much more. I went to many of these activities always looking for something but it was very hard to find as I didn't know exactly what it was that I was looking for so how on earth was I to know when I found it!

Actually, perhaps in fact we are never meant to "find" the truth or ultimate answer because if and when we do, or think we do, then somehow we cease growing or learning or becoming who and what we really are. Because maybe in us trying to find out who and what we are the Universe and Creation also can find out more about who and what they are?

At that time I was more concerned with finding out more about who and what I was, because somehow after so many years of stilted and systemised education I knew that whoever and whatever I thought I was that wasn't me or certainly not the all of me.

I therefore began to go to lots of different groups, meetings and events in this search to find the "me" that had gone missing. I also began to read in a way that I had never read before, from my own need rather than someone or something else's need.

In New Zealand I had always been taught English by incredibly boring teachers who brought no life, passion or joy to literature, but instead told us that we had to read the classics and know how to answer questions about them because there would be an exam on them at the end of the year.

This continued at University where studying law for the best part of five years meant reading endless textbooks and memorising hundreds of cases in order that they could be regurgitated at the end of the year so that another exam could be passed and ticked off the list on my way to becoming ...... a lawyer!

After about 20 years of this type of education I had developed something of an allergy to reading because of the way it was foisted upon me. But now, because I had a real hunger and need to find what I didn't know I was looking for I began to read passionately and diversely on all sorts of topics and subjects, themes and genres.

It was like I had only been eating beetroot all my life and now I discovered all sorts of exotic fruits and vegetables from all round the world. This was also literally true as I began to explore all sorts of different foods that were available in London's markets!

Anyway, the point of all this preamble is that one of the first books I read in my newly discovered bibliophile phase was by Jiddhu Krishnamurti.

It was called: *As One is: To Free the Mind from All Conditioning.*

Quite an appropriate title considering where I was in my own journey at the time. There was something very special about this book for me; not so much in the words themselves in the book (although they were quite amazing in themselves) but something, somehow in the spaces between the words. There was something intimate, kind, soft, feminine somehow that allowed me to breathe a different kind of breath; a breath that didn't just fill the top third of my lungs but somehow reached almost every cell of my body.

It was then I realised that most of my every day, general life experience was based not in my body but in my brain. For that is where most if not all of my education had been based. Training my brain to better become what I wasn't and then thinking that what I wasn't was in fact me.

No wonder I was confused!

Krishnamurti's writing helped me come back to me, or at least begin that journey back to myself. I so wanted his book to have all the answers I thought I needed and perhaps for him to be the guru I was looking for but alas it wasn't quite like that. For what I began to discover was that in reality no person can truly lead another, for that means that the other is no longer free. We may help each other find our true selves but a true leader may shine a light for another but they never seek to be or become the other's light.

I was just happy to read Jiddhu's words and feel their wisdom which felt as though they didn't belong to him but that he had somehow found them and wanted to share them with me. And that felt good, settling and comforting and somehow gave me access to parts of myself that I didn't know I had.

It is therefore fitting that I choose a quotation from Krishnamurti for this book, for it is a lovely one, and one I can acknowledge and verify from my own experience of the words.

Once one is able to quieten and listen, the incessant noise in the head that is forever trying to control one's experience of reality a new kind of reality manifests.

A whole new series of feelings, emotions, awareness, knowings, consciousness and therefore reality emerges. When we let go of the fear of letting go of the fear then what are we left with is love. And love touches depths within us that fear simply doesn't have the ability to touch. No wonder fear is scared! ☺

It is what keeps us from giving and receiving love. It even has a name believe it or not – Philophobia – the fear of being in love and falling in love.

What a terrible fear to have especially in the light of the fact that we are all upheld, supported and loved by the whole Universe in how it arranged itself so precisely just so that we could experience its magnificence and beauty.

What's not to love about that?

Where the Mind is biggest, the Heart, the Senses, Magnanimity, Charity, Tolerance, Kindliness, and the rest of them scarcely have room to breathe.

Virginia Woolf

Often in history art has represented the human form in specific ways to emphasise the importance of a particular feature or features that the artist wished to convey to the observer as being important.

For example, in the very earliest representations of the earth goddess from pre-historic times the figure has extremely large breasts and it is thought that she was represented in this way to emphasise her fertility and life giving and life affirming properties.

The mother goddess who gives life to and sustains all. She who gives birth, nourishes and engages in a profound way with the cycles of life and living.

The above picture is called The Venus of Dolni Vestonice and is thought to be up to 30,000 years old.

As can be seen from the picture, the size of the breasts and the hips are disproportionately large as if to insist that the viewer focuses on them rather than say the face and the head which are predominantly featureless.

It was in all probability regarded as some sort of divine, religious artefact by those who made it and was possibly an object of veneration for the culture it came from as they sought ways to understand the world they lived in, how nature worked and how they could interpret the world and possibly influence nature and it events.

It certainly shows that these early humans knew and felt that life couldn't and shouldn't be understood through a literal representation of the world that they found themselves in, but that there were subtleties, nuances, unknown and mysterious influences and perceptions.

They had needs to survive and flourish like all other forms of organic life on Earth, but unlike other species on earth these early humans knew that their lives were governed by external forces and sometimes these influences aided and provided for their needs and other times they brought events like droughts, floods, famines, plagues that made their lives difficult in the extreme.

In understanding that their lives were influenced by these external events this meant that they could begin to think about how they themselves might begin to influence and shape the events that influenced them.

This is where it would appear that we begin to find the beginnings of things like rites, rituals, ceremonies and worshipping of objects, deities, nature and the like begin to appear in the human story.

These early humans began to develop the faculty of perception in a much deeper way and they could start to represent their experience and what was important to them in producing objects that weren't just functional like tools such as axes, spears, knives, fishing hooks, bowls and so on. They began to produce what we would today call art in the broadest sense of that term.

Who really knows what The Venus of Dolni Vestonice meant to the person who was carving it and why they carved it in the way that they did? What were they thinking? What were they trying to capture? What did it mean to the fellow members of their tribe and culture? What ceremonies and rites did they have around what the goddess was meant to represent to them? What prayers and incantations did they make to the *"gods and goddesses"* of which she may have been one?

It is clear that they felt it was important to represent something or someone from their world as they perceived it, something that was significant in and for their lives perhaps in the hope that by creating an external focus that that could somehow play a part in influencing events from fertility, to the weather, to the seasons and so on.

These matters were clearly in their contemplations but they cannot have formed part of what we modern humans would call rational thinking because human beings cannot influence external events like the seasons or the weather, can we?

Well maybe in fact we can, because for example today we clearly do influence the weather with everything going on regarding human activities affecting and causing climate change for example from deforestation to air pollution and CO_2 emissions and so on.

Perhaps those ancient people felt they could and did in fact influence their world too?

They no doubt looked for clues in the subtle changes of the seasons and the events that shaped their lives and tried to find ways to cause things that they wanted and needed to happen to occur. Much in the same way, if not necessarily using the same methodologies, that we do today.

For whilst today we have many millions if not billions of people who pray to their god or gods for what they want or need, we also have many millions or billions of people who have the power and ability to shape their world, and they do, using far more powerful external technologies and on a far greater scale that our ancient ancestors did.

This is because the human "mind" and its capabilities to conceive of and build things outside has grown in an exponential and quantum way since those early humans carved The Venus of Dolni Vestonice all those millennia ago.

What would the person who carved The Venus of Dolni Vestonice make of the Empire State Building, the Three Gorges dam in China or Heathrow Airport? Would our culture make any more sense to them than theirs makes to us?

It is hard to see that ours would make any sense to them whatsoever, whereas we can at least have an inkling about theirs in terms of their hopes, fears, beliefs and practices and of course their basic human needs for things like food, water, air, warmth and shelter.

It is clear that the human mind has expanded its reach and possibilities beyond any conceivable notion that the ancient peoples who made those carvings could have imagined.

Yet one wonders once they have got over their sheer incredulity and awe at the scale and complexity of our modern human ingenuity would they be left with a question regarding it all of: "Why?" For what ultimate purpose do these objects serve and what reason and value do these things have to the meaning of human lives and their existence?

Is it a better and deeper reason than they had for carving a simple earth goddess?

Perhaps these are some of the things that Virginia Woolf might be alluding when she speaks of the danger of the mind becoming too big and too dominant over other faculties?

The Irish have an expression that perhaps captures this well when they say to be careful that in running after things that you don't lose the run of yourself.

An obvious example where this is concerned is money and the things that people will do to get it. And yet money itself is no more real than the Tooth Fairy, Santa Clause, The Easter Bunny and Abominable Snowman. OK, OK I'll admit that one of those does actually exist but I'm not saying which one!

What would our ancestors of 30,000 years ago say if we produced before their eyes a million dollars and told them this is one of the most desired objects in our culture and that some people literally worship it and dedicate their lives to the pursuit of getting as much of it as they can.

Would it make any sense to them? It is highly doubtful that it could or would, because their minds would not have any concept of money whatsoever, nor would they be able to use it for anything practical in their world order.

The same could be said for things like space rockets. For many scientists like to trumpet the fact that we have developed the scientific capacity to build a machine that enables us to escape the atmosphere of our home planet and to stay away for perhaps months at a time. This is often lauded as one of the greatest achievements of our species and our development.

But is it?

For ultimately it is just metal, plastic, nuts and bolts, glass and fuel, all stuck together in a reasonably stable but fragile form that hopefully holds itself together as it flies through space. It also contains a little bit of the Earth's atmosphere plus food because there isn't either of them in space.

One could easily ask the question of our so called *"giant leap for mankind"* what's the point?

Our ancestors certainly wouldn't be able to put such a rocket to any practical use or purpose and it is questionable whether we can either.

One wonders if given the choice whether our ancient carver would choose a space rocket, the Empire State Building or The Venus of Dolni Vestonice?

Whilst we can never know for sure it is highly likely he (or she) would choose The Venus of Dolni Vestonice because it has tangible meaning to his or her life. For in their mind it represents something real, important and relevant to their lives.

The mind has an incredible capacity for invention, knowledge and achievement. But without a framework and a context it can both tend to run away with itself and become dominant over other faculties that equally if not more importantly define who and what we are as individuals and as a species.

Therefore before we judge the carver of The Venus of Dolni Vestonice as being "primitive" let us think for a moment and reflect on our own so called progress.

For can we live without The Empire State Building and a space rocket? The answer is that we most certainly can for we lived without them for 99.9999% of the time since someone sat down with a piece of stone and decided to carve the Venus of Dolni Vestonice.

But can we live without magnanimity, charity, tolerance and kindness? The answer is that we possibly / probably can but our experience as human would be much lesser without them than they would if we didn't have the Empire State Building and a space rocket.

And when one looks at The Venus of Dolni Vestonice and spends some time with it and wonders what the person who made it had in their mind, then somehow, perhaps one feels more of that magnanimity, charity, tolerance and kindness than one would ever get from a space rocket that seeks to take us away from who and what we really are.

Who is calling who Primitive?

It is said that often the solution to a dilemma is a case of mind over matter.

That may well be true, but it is important to keep in mind what one is being mindful of when one is trying to overcome what one perceives the matter to be!

In real terms, is the journey within towards the truth of what one really is any less infinite than the journey to the furthest star 13.8 billion light years away on the other side of the Universe?

And are we any closer to our destination than the person who carved that piece of rock and poured his or her love, belief and values into it all those years ago?

Educating the mind without educating the heart is no education at all.

Aristotle

Aristotle lived in Ancient Greece from about 384-322 B.C. although what year they called the ones they lived then in is not entirely clear as the B.C. that we in the West use for the calendar today takes as its year zero the purported birth year of Jesus Christ. But since Christ was not born for nearly another 400 years after Aristotle was born they would hardly have told friends that "I was born in 384 B.C." unless they were perhaps the Nostradamus of their day.

However, they wouldn't have known of Nostradamus either would they because he wasn't born until 1503 A.D. Unless possibly they were the Old Mother Shipton of their day but then she wasn't born until .... Oh dear!

Anyway, Aristotle was born a long, long time ago and is regarded by many as being the father of modern science. He certainly appears to be the first person to apply the principles of what we might understand today as being the scientific method in that he looked to develop experimental methods whereby facts and findings could be ascertained to determine the truth or otherwise of a theory being postulated.

The name Aristotle actually means *"The best purpose"* which is a rather wonderful and fitting name for someone who had such an enquiring and penetrating mind and whose range of studies and teachings transcended many realms and subjects from science to philosophy to mathematics to morals and ethics to politics and much more.

He was also Alexander the Great's teacher, and it is doubtful if Alexander would have been as great as he was without Aristotle providing him with his teaching, guidance and moral compass, although it has to be said that Alexander didn't always follow Aristotle's teachings to the exact letter when conquering lands that resisted his invasions.

Nevertheless, Aristotle's teachings were hugely influential on Alexander and helped shaped his own beliefs and philosophy, and without those teachings he may well have ended up as being Alexander the Average or Alexander the Forgotten.

Not only did Aristotle influence Alexander in shaping his views but he also influenced the whole study of subjects like science and philosophy for many centuries to come and even right down to the one we live in today. In fact, his influence was so strong, particularly in the Middle Ages when his work was largely rediscovered and re-invigorated, that to disagree with Aristotle was tantamount to heresy.

His teachings became dogma which is rather ironic to say the least because the whole point of his scientific method was to test theories against the truth of nature and her laws and see what the evidence actually said about the theory.

It is often said that with Aristotle began the formal study of logic and reason in that theories needed to be tested if at all possible against observable facts.

Although that isn't to say that he himself didn't develop what we would today call some wacky theories. For example, he believed in spontaneous generation, that the Earth was eternal and unchanging and that the only place that change happened was in a region between the Earth and the Moon, that fossils came from an inorganic origin i.e. that they were never living organisms, that heavier objects like rocks fell faster to the Earth because they had more earth in them than lighter objects which took longer to fall because they had more air in them, and also he believed that women were basically deformed men! Bad, naughty Aristotle!

Despite these errors, Aristotle did believe in the primacy of the senses and what they detected and observed as being the best methodology of discovering the truth. Although it cannot be said that he always applied the scientific method in the rigorous way that modern scientists would recognise today. For example, he claimed that men and women had a different number of teeth. Yet any simple examination of the mouths of men and women who still had all their teeth would have shown him that this clearly wasn't the case!

So whilst his methods weren't perhaps as rigorous as those we know today, he certainly believed that one should try and get objective corroboration if possible of what the case actually was, and this was best done by what one observed through the five senses.

Thomas Aquinas (who was one of the major advocates of Aristotle's teachings in the Middle Ages that led to his views and philosophy being so powerful and persuasive) said of Aristotle's method that:

"Nothing was in the intellect that not first in the senses."

Notwithstanding the errors of both his approach and some of his methods, the template that he established for the scientific approach in discovering the truth was nothing short of remarkable. His *History of Animals* (where he described, dissected and classified over 500 animals) was nothing like any previous work that had gone before, and therefore in some ways it is not hard to see why his work became the authoritative treatise for the best part of 24 centuries on so many subjects. He was a true polymath in the deepest meaning of that word.

His work paved the way for Darwin and his theory of natural selection in evolution and so it is perhaps not surprising that Darwin would say the following of Aristotle:

"Linnaeus and Cuvier have been my two gods, though in very different ways, but they were mere school-boys to old Aristotle."

Clearly Aristotle wasn't just about educating the mind as the quote at the start of this chapter clearly shows.

He clearly felt that what we would call academic learning wasn't enough for a person to "know" something.

"All men by nature desire to know." he said.
But know what?
And by what nature?

He knew that there was both and inner and an outer nature to "man" and that we need to develop both aspects equally in order to discover the truth.

The outer nature of the truth could be better discerned by observing nature and how it worked and learning from those methods in order to organise human life, both individually and collectively.

We should also observe our own inner nature to find the deeper meaning of our lives by finding the correct philosophical, moral and ethical principles in order to conduct ourselves properly and fairly in line with those inner truths whatever we discover them to be.

Again it is little wonder that this inner and outer truth discovery process had such a profound influence for so long because no one before Aristotle had managed to marry and synthesise the scientific and philosophical and religious aspects of living in such a comprehensive (if not always accurate) and compelling way.

But in setting out the template for the scientific method we know today Aristotle is clearly also issuing a warning against the dominance of the mind over the heart.

Knowing something is one thing, but feeling it is quite another.

Knowing, or thinking one knows, what love is is one thing, but being in love and loving and be loved are quite something different. Analysing what a great painting is one thing but being moved by it is the point of its existence.

It seems that Aristotle is suggesting that affairs of the heart aren't purely instinctive or automatic because he is intimating in the quote that the heart just like the mind can be educated.

This seems to suggest that Aristotle truly was well ahead of his time (if that doesn't sound like modernist, revisionist, condescension!) for it appears that he most certainly was aware of the importance of a balance between the nature and nurture sides of ourselves and that one shouldn't dominate the other.

Both sides are needed to find the true essence of things as they really are because both sides go to make up the essence of who and what **we** are. He may not have used the terms nature and nurture, but his philosophy certainly carries the awareness that there were these two sides to human nature.

He was always seeking the Universal within his researches and methods and unlike his teacher Plato, who believed that the Universal lay separate and outside the particular of specific things and influenced them as an outside force, Aristotle believed that the Universal existed **within** the particular thing itself and could be found if one knew how to find its essence or being.

He very much carried the sentiment of – if you want to understand the Universe study man and if you want to understand man study the Universe.

It is interesting that Aristotle left Plato's school after Plato died and the school was taken over by Plato's nephew. It is said that Aristotle did not like the direction the school then took in that it became more and more about fixed rules and teachings. He wanted to be free to explore the nature of things as they truly are for himself.

Yet ironically again his own findings became a very similar kind of fixed truth for many centuries afterwards up until the time of the Enlightenment when his theories and findings came to be challenged by the scientific method and empiricism.

And whilst Aristotle would possibly marvel at some of scientific methods and methodologies we have today he may seek to remind us of his quote about the mind and the heart.

For educating the mind about particle physics, quantum theory, string theory, M theory, Big Bang and The Higgs Boson won't ever find compassion, hope or kindness because they don't live in that finite world of stuff as we know it.

They live in the infinite world of what Aristotle's name literally means – The Best Purpose.

Perhaps Aristotle within all his findings, teachings and philosophy was in simple terms saying that each person can find their best purpose if they have the right and proper education.

And in order to have the right education a person needs to observe the world outside themselves as it really is and learn from it. They also need to look inside themselves and especially their heart and find out what they too are really like and learn from that too.

Aristotle may have got some things wrong, but it would appear that he got some very, very big things right.

There never was any heart truly great and generous that was not also tender and compassionate.

Robert Frost

It is often said that opposites attract and in some respects this is true. For the positive end of a magnet attracts the negative end of another magnet in that as they get closer and closer there comes a moment when this attractive force becomes so powerful so that not only do they attract each but they are pulled together in what can only be described as a compulsive force. They are attracted to each other so much so that they cannot not be together and when joined they no longer are two things but become a complete, new one thing.

The analogy is often drawn that things that appear perhaps at first glance to be polar opposites are attracted to each and this is particularly applied to couples who appear to be very different. For example, one partner in the couple may be extrovert and the other introvert, one may quiet and reserved whilst the other may be a social networker and talk for Ireland and lots of small countries.

This gives rise to the expression that opposites attract.

But are such things in fact truly opposites in the literal meaning of that term?
Because the word opposite derives its meaning from the word oppose and to oppose something means to be against it, to resist it, to stand in the way of something, to seek to impede or hinder its growth or progress.

If the phrase that "opposites attract" is used with this context and meaning then it suggests that this doesn't create the platform for a successful relationship. Whilst it may be true that some relationships based on the principle of "opposites attract" are in conflict, the deeper meaning of the term suggests that the two natures are in fact complementary and indeed create a stronger bond than if the two natures were kept apart.

They do not have to be forced to be together but something within the attractive force at play between the two forces suggests that they belong together in a way that two things that are not charged or attracted just sit side by side with no bond between them joining because there is no mutual attraction.

This is true when all things in nature, including humans, seek a partner. They are seeking some kind of bond and they often go through what are often elaborate courtship procedures to see if there is a sufficient mutual attraction to create some kind of bond and attachment that may lead to mating and rearing young together and often much more. Before cementing this bond there may be all sorts of ritual displays from nest building, to courtship displays to dancing and in the case of humans perhaps going to the movies and sharing a bag of popcorn and maybe a bit more in the back row!

In can be seen that there is a whole process that exits within nature where the deeper truth of the statement "opposites" attract" is in fact that "birds of a feather flock together".

This statement is obviously true because when for example one sees a flock of starlings of possibly 10,000 birds swirling and swooping in incredible aerial displays one doesn't see pigeons, albatross, owls or seagulls all joining in the flock. Nor does one see impala, lions and hippos joining a herd of wildebeest as they begin their annual migration nor lots of different species of fish joining the salmon on their migration up the rivers and streams to their spawning grounds.

Nor does one see different species seeking out and partnering and mating with other species. Pink flamingos tend to breed with and congregate with other pink flamingos. Elephants tend to stick with other elephants, wombats tend to like other wombats and goodness knows why but even sloths are attracted to each other!

The common thread within this force of attracting a mate or partner is that each party is looking for a good catch. By good catch it is meant that consciously or unconsciously one party is looking for certain qualities in the other whether that be bright plumage, big tusks, a long neck or even a good sense of humour.

This sense of opposites attracting each other and performing complementary roles or functions was encapsulated in the childhood nursery rhyme I remember when my mother would encourage us to leave nothing wasted on their plate at the end of the meal:

Jack Sprat could eat no fat.
His wife could eat no lean.
And so between them both, you see,
They licked the platter clean.

Perhaps the rhyme may be seen these days as not entirely politically correct but it did and still does convey the sense of lives complementing each other's needs and capabilities rather than mirroring them or imitating them.

After all a football team with 11 strikers in the starting line-up isn't going to win many matches. They may score quite a few goals but the odds are that in a complete absence of any defence whatsoever they are going to let in far more goals than they score! Nor for that matter is a team of 11 goalies going to win many games either. They may manage a few 0-0 draws with 11 goalies on the goal line keeping out most attempts on goal, but they are bound to let the odd one in here and there and they certainly aren't going to score any at the other end!

Perhaps there is something deeper behind this idea of apparent opposites attracting each other that suggests that rather than opposites attracting it is in fact sameness that is doing the attracting. For if we fully subscribe to the view that it is opposites that are attracting each other then that would lead to the view that men and women are in fact opposite to each other and therefore oppose each other.

That is obviously a ridiculous view, for no culture can survive without the genders finding a way to co-exist and co-operate successfully together. Yet if one looks closely at world history and even in many cultures in our world today including our so called emancipated West, it is clear that many times in many cultures the relationship has not been viewed (particularly by men it has to be said) as an equal and collaborative one.

It is when the apparent opposites change their perceptions about each other that the nature of the relationship changes and deepens into a one with much greater mutuality, respect and a different order of need. Not need of what one wants to get from the other but what one can achieve **with** the other. This is clearly what attracts them to each other in the first place, or at least does so if the attraction is a natural one.

If the qualities that one is attracted to in another (for this is what natural attraction is based upon from physical features to personal attributes) then the attractive qualities are generally not singular but usually multiple in the way that Robert Frost is describing in the quotation.

It is doubtful that we are ever attracted to another person for just one reason or quality even if we might think that there may be only one. Unconsciously we are measuring and registering multiple frequencies (for that is what they truly are) and making choices upon those registrations.

As birds of a feather flock together then so it would be with qualities in that a great and generous heart would also be tender and compassionate. Because if the heart of the person wasn't tender and compassionate then how could it possibly be regarded as being great and generous? To be great and generous and harsh and uncaring are clearly polar opposites and they certainly don't attract each other because they are inconsistent and mutually exclusive.

It is therefore impossible to be two opposite things at the same time.

There are of course the obvious things that are clear opposites that proves that this is true. For example, one can't be cruel and kind at the same time despite the popular saying that one has to be cruel to be kind. If one is being cruel to a child or a partner or an animal, then one certainly isn't being kind to them.

Other examples include love and hate. People sometimes say that they have a love / hate relationship with something or another person. Well it's not possible to occupy both camps of this duality at the same moment in time and if one is fluctuating between the two states on a regular basis then it certainly isn't the formula for a successful long term relationship with anyone or anything.

What seems to be the case is that rather than opposites being attracted it is in fact the case that similar things attract each other and not only that but these things are not singular but rather multiple.

It is said that you can know what someone is like but who their friends are.
It is also said that one should choose their friends wisely.

It would therefore seem that both statements are true and that the heart is the place to hold dear and true the things, people and qualities that make the human generous of spirit, countenance and action.

The things that we love in our heart tell us what we are.

St. Thomas Aquinas

St Thomas Aquinas was a 13th century Dominican priest and friar and is regarded by the Catholic Church as one of the most esteemed and important philosophers and theologians in all its history.

His influence on modern philosophy and theology is immense for in many ways he bridged the ancient world of Aristotle and the modern world of today with his sometimes radical and pioneering thinking on subjects from theology to philosophy to ethics to liturgy and canon law to metaphysics and political theory and more.

He even had a philosophical school of thought named after him – Thomism which incorporates many of his understandings, views and beliefs on the meaning of existence, God, humanity and morality. He was an extremely capable and profound thinker and synthesiser of philosophical and religious teaching and was able to bring these sometimes disparate views into a coherent whole that combined the mundane and simple with the complex theological and philosophical arguments about the meaning and purpose of life.

Indeed, so important did the Church regard Thomas's teachings and philosophies that they adopted them as being their own as stated by Pope Benedict XV in the early 20th century. And if the Church adopts your teachings into their dogma then you clearly have made the top division of political, religious and secular thinking. This is especially so if they make you a Saint as well!

His main writing that we know of today is Summa Theologica within which he sets out many of his findings on all matters to do with the host and hosanna of human experience. It is hard to overestimate Thomas's influence on medieval thinking and that influence extends to even today. The Second Vatican Council in the 1960's termed Thomas's system as being the "Oerennial Philosophy". High praise for someone who had died nearly 700 years earlier.

People may today disagree with Thomas's his views on some or all the matters he addressed, but they rarely ignore him. His influence is in many ways as strong as that of Aristotle and that is not really that surprising since Thomas was highly influenced indeed by Aristotle's thinking and approach in what could be called natural theology.

Of the many things Thomas addressed he sought to discover the nature of things unto themselves i.e. what is the essence or the being-ness of a thing and secondly the reason for what that thing exists and what caused that thing to exist in the first place and for what purpose? If that purpose could be known or understood, does that, or could that give a tangible and real argument for the fact that a first cause or first causer i.e. God, exists?

The arguments put forward by Thomas are many, varied and at times very complex but they do cross many boundaries from science to philosophy to religion and theology which is why his arguments have sustained for so long and are still relevant today, particularly due to the fact that the Catholic Church still endorses many of them.

So what is the nature of a thing unto itself?
What makes it what it is?
What caused it to come into being?
For what purpose or reason did the "causer" cause it to
come into existence?
And who or what is the causer?

These are obviously huge and deeply profound questions
and contemplations and Thomas addressed them in both
scientific and philosophical terms.

It is also important to remember that Thomas lived 600
years before Darwin and Wallace posited their theory of
natural selection in evolution which suggests that
species evolve over long periods of time and adapt
according to the changes in their environment. By this
process of natural selection those who are most
beneficially adapted get to pass on their genes to the next
generation. This ensures that the species has the best
chance possible of both surviving and adapting. There
are no guarantees however that a species will survive as
the fact that over 99% of species that have ever lived on
Earth are now extinct proves.

Bearing in mind that Thomas was unaware of the
process of natural selection and that he probably didn't
think that species evolved, does his theory of approach to
the essence of things hold up or at least provide a
platform for his other theories and philosophical
arguments?

Many scientists today would argue that they don't,
because the essence or nature of a thing can only be
understood through using the scientific method to
discover what its constituent parts are and how they are
put together and how they work. And with things like

electron microscopes, centrifuges and the discovery of DNA and sub-atomic particles the essence of things can be better discovered than ever before.

But can they?

We all know what an apple is.
But what is it that makes it an apple?
What gives it its apple-ness?

We can all say something about what makes an apple an apple from looking at an actual apple – it is red if ripe, green if not, grows on trees, is round in nature, is usually about 3-5 inches in diameter, has a thinner, harder outer skin that is peel-able or can be bitten through to reveal a softer inner white flesh that is edible and an inner core that contains its seeds.

So we know in part at least at descriptive level what an apple is and why it exists, or at least part of why it exists. It exists in the form it does so that fauna life (like we humans) will eat it and when we later scatter the seeds of the apple away from the tree where it grew and therefore we increase the chances of the apple tree continuing its species by the seeds taking root and growing another apple tree.

Thomas Aquinas may not have known all of the science that we know about an apple as stated above, but he would still have known what an apple was and part of why it existed and that the seeds if planted produced another apple tree.

Was Thomas Aquinas further removed from the essence of what an apple is because he didn't know about evolutionary theory, gene theory, quantum theory and sub-atomic theory?

He probably didn't understand the biological and genetic processes at play at microscopic level to do with chemical and biological processes and the relationships between things like proteins, amino acids, polymer chains and so on, and he wouldn't have been able to genetically sequence an apple to see how it was genetically differently from an orange.

But this doesn't necessarily mean that Thomas was further away from the essence of what an apple is. For if one gets further and further into the micro worlds of the constituent elements of the apple one gets to the point that one can no longer see the apple for the trees!

At sub-atomic level physicists no longer argue about what the essence of an apple is but whether string theory or M theory or multiverse theory or countless other theories should be preferred in explaining what the nature of reality looks like.

Sometimes one can lose the substance by grasping at the shadow.

Seeking to capture the essence of something by describing its constituent parts in greater and greater and ever minuter detail doesn't actually tell us what it is, what its purpose is and why it exits in the first place. The fact that an apple is made up of a unique genetic sequence of ACGT doesn't get us any closer to its "being". In fact, it takes us further away.

What gets us closer to the "being" of an apple is when we see it, touch, it, smell it, taste it and hear that unique crunch type noise when we bite into it.

Thomas Aquinas knew that rational thought and logic alone couldn't explain or reveal the full or all of the nature of things, although it could clearly reveal a lot.

Deductive reasoning alone isn't enough to explain the nature of things. There is also an inductive and a transcendent part to reality that can only be understood through faculties that are higher than dissection and analysis.

But what faculties are these because science would say that if they don't exist materially then they don't exist at all?

Thomas Aquinas would use terms like faith, belief, knowing, prayer, love, kindness, generosity and so on.

Are these faculties or are they processes of other faculties that we have in the brain? Or perhaps the mind?

Thomas is giving us a clue when he says the things that we love in our hearts tell us who we are. He is not saying it is the things we think in our heads even though in his day people knew that thinking was a mental process and that that was done in the head with the brain.

Thomas says that there are higher processes that in fact define who and what we are. It's not the fact that we are carnal beings who eat, drink, breathe, procreate and die that define our experience as human beings. It is what we love, what we care about, what we believe in, what we are devoted to, what we cherish, what we are grateful for, who and what we give thanks to and so much more.

Science in some ways is in fact catching up with Thomas Aquinas for it is now being discovered that what we think, do, believe and have faith in affects our very being.

There may or may not be a God but scientific studies have shown that people who have faith and believe in a higher being and / or purpose tend to live longer, healthier and happier lives than those who do not.

This doesn't prove that any such higher being or purpose does or doesn't exist, but what it does prove is that if you do genuinely (no faking now!) believe there is such a purpose then at least you have a better chance of hanging around for longer to find out whether there is or there isn't!

What you love reveals who and what you are because you become what you think about and you are what you love.

String theory doesn't explain what love is although you may have fallen in love when the strings in the orchestra were playing your song and it touched both your hearts. In that particular scenario thank goodness for strings!

You may love truth, justice, beauty, fairness, honour, joy, kindness, simplicity. If you do, then that reveals who and what you are.

You might think that you love pizza, but you don't actually love it, you like it. And maybe if you like it too much then you start to look like one too, for not only do you become what you think about, but you are what you eat, and you are what you love.

The ascendant knowledge we can gather about the nature of things and how they work can reveal much about what we are and how we got here.

The transcendent feelings, knowings, loves and feelings we experience can also reveal who and what we can be if only we open up our hearts and let the sunshine in (and out).

Your vision will become clear only when you can look into your own heart. Who looks outside, dreams; who looks inside, awakes.

Carl Jung

Nice one Carl! ☺

As most people know Carl Jung was, along with Sigmund Freud, an eminent pioneer of psychoanalysis in the early and middle parts of the 20th century.

Although Freud was older than Jung their careers still overlapped and for quite a while they were collaborators and held similar views about their field of expertise.

They first met in 1907 and worked together for about six years and set up the International Psychoanalytic Association together in 1911.

However, as they got older their views diverged, particularly in Jung's view due to the fact that Freud tended to be somewhat trenchant and dogmatic in his views and wouldn't tolerate any opinions or theories that differed from his own.

Jung from the time of their split very much pursued his own methods and techniques of psychoanalysis until he established a very different school to Freud that is still used today as Jungian Analysis.

Without wishing to bottom line the differences between the two men and their approaches to psychoanalysis, partly because some of their differences were in fact personal as much as professional, Freud tended to favour a more empirical, fact based, more scientific and systematic approach to analysis whereas Jung tended to believe that there were more ways to understand the human mind and psyche than simply by using the so called natural sciences.

He was therefore much more prepared than Freud to look at things like dreams, myths and folklore as forming part of people's conscious and unconscious experience and even later in his life carried out many studies on subjects like astrology to try and ascertain whether it did have any influence on people's lives.

Freud regarded such studies as being a complete waste of time and totally unscientific. Jung on the other hand found things within his study of such things as astrology as being fascinating. He even expressed a regret later in his life saying that he wished he had spent more time studying astrology than he did psychoanalysis.

Perhaps Freud's approach to the subject can be seen to be more left hemisphere of the brain inclined (clinical) whereas that of Jung could be seen to be more right hemisphere (imaginative) inclined?

If anything, Freud tended to over simplify matters from a systems point of view and Jung tended to come up with theories that weren't always testable from an empirical standpoint. As such it could be easy to come up with "evidence" that tended to support the theory because the theory needed "evidence" to prove that the theory was right!

One of the concepts that Jung developed within his theory or model was that of the collective unconscious –

a term that we use today in many different contexts and meanings. To Jung it meant that the individual is influenced by many things within their own unconscious mind from the group or collective mind. As a result, the individual is shaped and formed by these processes in many ways that they themselves do not know about directly for the very reason that by definition they are – unconscious.

Because they are unconscious, they cannot really be tested by conscious testing methodologies, but in Jung's view they can be observed and noted.

Jung believed that this was essential in understanding the whole person, and that the unconscious mind was probably more important and influential in the development of the psyche of the person. Also the effective communication and connection between the conscious and unconscious parts of the person needed to be established in order to achieve full and proper "individuation" i.e. the attainment of self.

Jung believed that the collective unconscious was filled with what he called archetypes, or what we might call roles or stereotypes, and that the person needed to understand how these affected them and played themselves out in the person in order that they could better understand why they were the way were. This could then help them to change so that they may better reclaim the self of themselves and achieve "answers" to the fundamental questions of life such as happiness, the meaning of life and even spiritual fulfilment and dealing with issues such as fear.

Freud on the other hand believed in treating such "woolly" matters as spirituality and archetypes as both unprofessional and beyond the scope and brief of the psychoanalyst. In his view, every condition could be traced back to an identifiable cause and this usually related to some untreated and unresolved cause that could then be treated. In that sense he was a reductionist in that causes began and remained in the known and conscious worlds it was simply a matter of proper diagnosis (like any medical condition) and once the diagnosis established the cause of the mind or mental condition then proper treatment (again just like a medical condition) could be prescribed.

This context hopefully helps in approaching the quote from Jung.

Within his system of psychoanalysis Jung was a deep believer in the maxim of the ancients as particularly encapsulated by the words written on the door of the cave where the Delphic Oracle resided of "Know Thyself".

To know thyself was the most empowering and enabling process a person could engage in, because by undertaking such a process a person could begin to understand all the things that influenced them and governed them in causing them to be the way they were and act the way they did.

If a person knew what these influences were and how they worked, then they could make more informed selections and choices in order to achieve better individuation.

This process required a person to seek better understanding and fulfilment, not by looking out into the world to see what they wanted as a first principle, but rather by looking inside themselves to discover and learn who and what they really are and what they are influenced by and how.

For Jung this required the person, in part at least, to look into their heart as well as their mind. It was important not just to look at things like thoughts and attitudes, but also feelings and emotions if a person was to discover themselves for real.

Because if a person looks outside of themselves to try and find themselves and what they want, then their life will enter a dream-like state in both a literal and figurative sense. This is because they are identifying themselves with things and desires that are outside of themselves, and so they become almost asleep to the truth of themselves. Accordingly, they never really awaken to who and what they really are and therefore who and what they can really be.

Jung is saying that without looking into their heart a person's vision and therefore view can only ever be hazy, blurred or dream like. It could be said that without this deep view into their soul a person can only ever end up living a zombie like existence. They will by default become a kind of automaton living a robotic existence that becomes subject to hidden archetypes that live in the collective unconscious and are only too ready, willing and able to occupy an unconscious host.

It is only by becoming conscious of the unconscious that a person can free themselves from the overlord government of these archetypes.

The way to become more conscious is for a person to look into their heart and see, not what they think but what they truly feel and what moves them. Perhaps in the Buddhist sense not what they desire but what they would want to set free in this world and in themselves.

The heart knows what the head can only theorize about.

Without a clear vision the truth and therefore the future can only be murky and muted. Things cannot be seen for what they truly are and therefore decisions about what is best to do is cloudy, confused and risky.

It's not the glasses or the binoculars that one needs to clean in order to see things and the future better, but in fact the soul. It is sometimes said that the eyes are the windows to the soul.

But surely the converse also applies in that the eyes are the windows **out** from the soul as well.

If the soul is clear about its role and function, then what our eyes see changes accordingly.

Perception changes reception.

We only see the truth our eyes and heart allow us to see.

If Jung was right, then our heart and soul allow us to see much, much more of the truth of the world and therefore ourselves.

Welcome therefore to Carl Jung's world of 360 degree, 3D and infra-red and ultra violet vision!

Coming to a real life cinema screen near you very soon indeed!

Sweet is the lore which nature brings;
Our meddling intellect
Mis-shapes the beauteous forms of things;-
We murder to dissect.

Enough of science and of art;
Close up these barren leaves;
Come forth, and bring with you a heart
That watches and receives

The Tables Turned
By William Wordsworth

William Wordsworth was an English poet who lived in the 18th and 19th centuries and is forever associated with the Lake District in England and his love of nature and its powers.

His life straddles the birth and rise of the Industrial Revolution which he himself saw as a disease and an abhorrence to nature and her beauty. Much of his poetry is a commentary of this perennial struggle between the laws and powers of nature and the rise of mankind's powers to shape and alter nature and its beauty to serve its economic and mercenary needs and greed.

Wordsworth was born in 1770, and many things that we associate with the rise of the Industrial Revolution appear around this time including the invention of the Spinning Jenny and the Steam Engine, the erection of the first cast iron arch bridge at Telford in Shropshire and many other processes that affected agriculture, manufacture and the production of goods and their transport including the building of canals to transport goods from place to place much quicker.

Along with Samuel Taylor Coleridge, a very close friend and collaborator, Wordsworth was largely responsible for launching what became known as the Romantic Age of English poetry. Much of this movement can be seen as a reaction to this perceived blind addiction to so called progress and the cost that this had to nature and our relationship with it.

In many ways the movement created by Coleridge and Wordsworth could be seen as a very much a forerunner of the Environmental Movement that emerged in the 1960's with what is often termed the Hippie Movement and the concerns that many felt at that time about the negative impact that human life was having on the planet and its and our future prospects.

Wordsworth was also a contemporary of William Blake and whilst there is no evidence that the two men knew each other or were influenced by each other's works, there are clear similar interests in considering the wholeness and inter-connectedness of things together with the ideal of the perfection of man and the attainment of spiritual fulfilment.

For Wordsworth, the road to this fulfilment lay within the relationship with nature and its beauty whereas for Blake the path lay much more through transcendent connection to the spiritual dimension and how that caused ecstatic and truly religious feelings in the person. This for him was the truth of God as made real.

Whilst having very different approaches to the relationship between the material and the spiritual realms, both men regarded the so called progress of the Industrial Revolution as being both a disease and an insult to nature, its beauty and the place of man within the natural order of things.

Because he wrote in such simple, earthy, naturalistic terms, much of Wordsworth's work was, and still is today, regarded as being simplistic, naïve and out of step with reality. Hence the labelling of it as being Romantic, which was and is an easy way of attempting to dismiss it.

The most famous of Wordsworth's poems is undoubtedly:

"I wandered lonely as a Cloud."

Its opening verse clearly illustrates both Wordsworth's style and how it is often regarded. There are not many children who haven't been taught the opening verse of the poem with its picture postcard imagery that sounds like it may have been written by the tourist office in Cumbria trying to get people to visit the area. They didn't write it but it certainly gets lot of people to visit the area that is for sure!

> *I wandered lonely as a cloud,*
> *That floats on high o'er vale and hill,*
> *When all at once I saw a crowd*
> *A host of golden daffodils*
> *Beside the lake, beneath the trees*
> *Fluttering and dancing in the breeze.*

Because of its ubiquity, it is easy to dismiss the poem as being twee, quaint, simplistic, unsophisticated, lightweight, shallow, naïve, childlike or even childish, and of course romantic.

Certainly Wordsworth was out of step with the nature of the revolution that was rapidly and inexorably changing the landscape of his times in a profound way both materially and philosophically.

Wordsworth was then, and still is today, regarded as being someone who looked back in time rather than forwards, and in looking back he romanticised as to what he thought life was like in the golden days of yore and ignored the harsh realities of times gone past. As such his views could be discounted and discarded as not being in step with current economic, social, political and scientific thinking.

He was regarded therefore as being something of an anachronism.

Yet if one looks within the content of his poems there is much to take note of in the warnings contained within them. The messages they carry for us today some 200 years later are just as relevant as they were then.

If one looks at the context of the times that Wordsworth lived in, it is possible to see that the seeds for the Industrial Revolution are sown some 100 years before within what has become known as The Enlightenment or The Age of Reason.

This was a time when hugely influential thinkers, philosophers and scientists such as Descartes, Bacon, Kant, Voltaire and Newton changed the landscape of the human race's relationship with nature and more importantly how we saw it and what we felt about it.

There was a profound shift in the centre of gravity from the heart to the head best summated by Descartes's immortal line: *I think therefore I am.*

This shift from the heart to the head or from feeling to thinking is evidenced with the change in thinking. Science, inventions and technological developments shift the focus away from our role with and within nature to much more one of how can we control, conquer and exploit nature for our own material ends.

With this shift of consciousness came greater yields and an increase in productivity and output which is why it came to be seen as "progress". But at the same time came huge side-effects from pollution to urbanisation, to poverty and diminishment of planetary resources that all continue today.

The reason that this continues is that the human race (in vast majority) has let the head rule the heart by suppressing and denying the heart's influence and importance in our relationships with the Earth and all the other species we share it with. It was the beginning of accelerated materialism in that we started to see things not in their wholeness and interconnectedness, but rather as things or objects that could be understood through understanding their constituent parts. The truth began to be seen in a reductionist rather than a holistic way and this justified the actions being undertaken in pursuit of so called progress because the mantra of the materialist is – the end justifies the means.

But for the holist – the end **is** the means. They are in fact inseparable from each other.

This was part of Wordsworth's philosophy and his message. That somehow in this lust for profits and progress the human race had created a schism between the heart and the head between both their internal nature and also the greater nature that they were somehow no longer an integrated part of.

Wordsworth himself stated his approach in his work The Recluse:

My voice proclaims
How exquisitely the individual Mind
(And the progressive powers perhaps no less
Of the whole species) to the external World
Is fitted:—and how exquisitely, too,
Theme this but little heard of among Men,
The external World is fitted to the Mind.

Powerful sentiments indeed, and perhaps fitting that he calls the work The Recluse as he himself was a recluse from the deafening din of the march of so called progress. Much in the same way that it regarded itself as being a recluse from him.

It is easy enough for the voice of "progress" to marginalise that which it sees as being out of step, romantic or even simply an impediment.

For where is the profit in romance?

Wordsworth seems to be suggesting that the relationship between the internal world and the external one has become badly damaged and broken and this is mainly because we have lost the ability to listen. For hearing something is very different to listening to that inner voice we all have within us.

Rather than going out and trying to lecture, persuade or change that outer noisy, disconnected and dispersed world, Wordsworth simply withdrew more and more from it and it was in and from that place he wrote The Recluse. It was a stance he chose, not because he wanted to be a recluse from his perception of the times he lived in, but one that was forced upon him because he felt there was no alternative to opting out of the Industrial Revolution and where it was heading.

So how do we learn how to listen in a deeper, more profound, connected way to the advice, counsels and wisdoms we need to hear before acting or reacting to the needs, problems and practicalities of life as it presents itself to us?

Wordsworth responds to this need within the poem The Tables Turned and so to end this chapter it is worth quoting the whole poem here and to then see what, if anything it says to you, the inner you reading it the best part of 200 years later and what order of resonance it perhaps causes.

It may be interesting before reading the poem to spend a couple of minutes feeling your pulse and then asking yourself the question – what does it actually mean to have a heart that watches and then receives?

The Tables Turned
An Evening Scene on the Same Subject

Up! up! my Friend and quit your books;
Or surely you'll grow double:
Up! up! my Friend, and clear your looks;
Why all this toil and trouble?

The sun above the mountain's head,
A freshening lustre mellow
Through all the long green fields has spread,
His first evening yellow.
Books! 'tis a dull and endless strife:
Come, hear the woodland linnet,
How sweet his music! on my life,
There's more of wisdom in it.
And hark! how blithe the throstle sings!
He, too, is no mean preacher:
Come forth into the light of things,
Let Nature be your Teacher.
She has a world of ready wealth,
Our minds and hearts to bless -
Spontaneous wisdom breathed by health,
Truth breathed by cheerfulness.
One impulse from a vernal wood
May teach you more of man,
Of moral evil and of good,
Than all the sages can.
Sweet is the lore which Nature brings;
Our meddling intellect
Mis-shapes the beauteous form of things: -
We murder to dissect.
Enough of Science and of Art;
Close up those barren leaves;
Come forth, and bring with you a heart
That watches and receives.

Every heart sings a song, incomplete, until another heart whispers back. Those who wish to sing always find a song. At the touch of a lover, everyone becomes a poet.

Plato

Plato lived at a time in ancient Greece and Athens at a time that is called the Golden Age of Greek scholarship and learning in the 4th and fifth centuries B.C. He was a student of Socrates and indeed much of his written work (in particular the body of work called The Dialogues) is based on the life of Socrates and his teachings.

It is therefore not easy to say what Plato's own beliefs and philosophy were because he very rarely writes in the first person, but is usually reporting the conversations or dialogues had with Socrates.

Plato was in turn the teacher of Aristotle at what was called the Academy where what was taught was termed Platonism (a term we still use today). Initially Aristotle was a devotee of Plato's philosophy, but after Plato's death Aristotle developed his own school of philosophy that diverted from Platonism and which came to be termed Empiricism. This then supplanted Platonism as the dominant influence in Western thought and teaching for the best part of 2,000 years.

Yet whilst Aristotle may have been the dominant influence in the shaping of philosophical and scientific traditions it has been said that everything that followed Plato has been mere footnotes to his philosophy and teachings.

To emphasise this point, we still have the term derived from his philosophy which we call Platonism. Platonism has waxed and waned in its influence in various cultures and schools of thought since the time of Plato. He has been in and out of fashion more times than all the clothes designers in the world combined!

He also gives his name to a particular type of relationship that we term platonic. Today it mainly means that it is a relationship based purely on friendship in that there is no direct sexual element within it. Originally however it meant much more than that, and we shall look at that in more detail shortly.

But what was and is Platonism?

Philosophers and thinkers have been arguing and debating exactly what Plato meant within his philosophy since his time. Not only that, but Platonism has evolved and changed over two millennia into such things as Middle Platonism and others versions such as Neo Platonism.

But perhaps the nub of what Platonism concerns itself with is – what is the nature of reality? Within that the question can be posed another question: – what is the reality of nature? For in order to be able to address the first question one needs to be able to answer the second one, and in order to answer the second question one needs to be able to answer the first!

One without the other only offers a glimpse, a segment, or perhaps at best a clue as to what lies behind the truth of the forms we see in the world and the perceptions we have about those forms.

Plato sought to address the contradiction inherent within the distinction between reality which is perceptible but is unintelligible, and reality which is intelligible and yet imperceptible to us.

The former appears to us in form and definition in the material world as abstractions of a higher truth, for nothing can appear unless it does so through a particular form. And the reason it appears in that particular form is that forms are immortal, even if we cannot understand the reason why those forms exist in the way that they do. Forms are eternal and unchanging and that is why things (animals, plant, humans etc.) appear in the forms that they do. (Bearing in mind that this is over 2,000 years before the time of Darwin).

On the other hand, reality exists on a much higher plane than we can perceive. If we can gain better perception about that higher reality, rather than just living in it, then life as it exists would become much more intelligible to us because we would know much more about why things are the way that they are rather than just accepting that they simply are that way period.

We can, and should, strive to know the mind of God or the gods, and if not the totality of same then at least more about it.

This struggle, search and endeavour to find the nature of reality continues very much today.

Does reality lie waiting to be discovered in the material worlds of science and cutting things up until we find their very essence or being? Or does in fact the truth become ever more unintelligible because the smaller and smaller the bits get the less and less we have of the whole?

Does the truth lie in much more ethereal, esoteric and philosophical realms that are mostly beyond our ken, because we don't have the mind capacity or development to look behind the corporeal veil and see the template behind their appearance and perhaps find greater truth there?

Darwin may have dealt a severe body blow to Plato's theory of forms, but nevertheless the essential axioms of Platonism remain intact inside the question – what is the nature of reality?

For whilst Darwinism states that organic life evolves by a process of natural selection, it doesn't tell us **why** they evolve, only how. In some senses Darwinism is simply is the other side of the coin of Platonism in that Platonism states that some things such as forms are immortal, whereas Darwinism states that nothing is immortal because everything is in flux.

The essential question therefore remains which is – can we make sense of our existence? Can we make it intelligible and meaningful, and perhaps even see if there is a purpose to it?

It seems that Plato has a fair point here, because if we just look at the world of *"things as they appear"* then when one gets down to the sub-atomic world of protons, neutrons, electrons, quarks and Higgs Bosons for example, how does one know that one is actually looking at the bits of a Duck Billed Platypus?

If on the other hand one goes to the other end of the spectrum and decides that nothing is in fact real and we are all living inside an imaginary hologram, then how do we feel pain?

Plato regarded the forms that exist in the world as being imperfect copies or archetypes of forms that exist in a higher plane. The highest of these perfect forms was The Form of Good and that all other forms had descended out of this one. He further taught that Good could be best understood through reason, but only if one first understood that the order of how things appeared from higher more perfected forms.

We cannot know truth through its imperfect forms as they appear in our world, we can only know the truth of the imperfect by knowing the perfect and the perfect is what is good.

This is a bit like the maxim that one can prove a greater truth with a lesser one.

Whilst Plato is a product of his time and his theories have come into and out of fashion there are still themes within his philosophy that resonate with us today. In some ways science and its discoveries confirm Plato's theories on the nature of reality and how we interpret it.

For example, the amazing discoveries within neuro-science and the processes of the brain confirm that we do indeed have complementary natures within our heads that give us different and sometimes contradictory interpretations of what reality looks like.

The left hemisphere of the brain would be much more akin to what Plato refers to as the imperfect world of forms that we inhabit, and how we see it to be in a very literal, physical and material sense. The right hemisphere of the brain is much more to do with the transcendent higher planes of consciousness and intelligence and is much more concerned with things like context, relationships, feelings, emotions, purpose and qualities.

Often the difference is explained by the analogy of the left side of the brain being more masculine inclined whereas the right side of the brain is more feminine in nature.

The relationship between the two sides of our experience is always a dynamic one and subject to flux and change in not only the individual, but also cultures and societies and indeed even different epochs.

In modern times, especially since the onset of the Industrial Revolution, the balance of power has shifted firmly and inexorably towards the left side of the brain being dominant over the right hand side.

Perhaps the truth of this shift can be seen in the James Brown song – It's a Man's World!

Certainly what can be seen is that in most if not all, first and second world countries at least and indeed many third world countries, they are dominated by men in almost every sphere of life, from politics to government to social control to education to religious influence and so on. Often the role of women is actively or indirectly marginalised and / or suppressed and they are rarely treated as equal partners.

This suggests an imbalance in the relationship between what Plato called the lower realm of forms and the higher one of causes, and what we might term the relationship between the two sides of the brain where one of which looks at things as commodities or objects and the other that looks at reasoning, context and process.

It is this higher side of our true nature, our being, our essence that reveals us as we really are. It is this aspect that allows us to love and be loved without possession or requirement and to love things for what and who they themselves truly are.

This is why we still have the term today of a platonic relationship or platonic love. It is a love that is much higher than simply a sexual relationship. It is pure, clean and transcends all known forms which is why it can exist above and beyond the "form" of gender.

It is a love that allows fulfilment and completion.

Perhaps this is place that Plato speaks of in his quote?

"Every heart sings a song, incomplete, until another heart whispers back."

Plato acknowledges that it is the heart or the inner part of our being that gives us access to this higher part of the truth that exists above and beyond the carnal. It is only through others that we give and receive this higher part of ourselves freedom and release.

What greater gift can a life receive than the knowing that one is received, valued and accepted?

"At the touch of a lover, everyone becomes a poet."

At the true level of what love really is, everyone can be a lover of the highest love of all which is the love of all that is good.

Plato doesn't say that at the touch of a lover everyone becomes a mathematician, an accountant or a statistician. Though to be fair he doesn't say such people are any less able to be touched by a lover than anyone else.

However, he specifically states that at the touch of a lover everyone becomes a poet.

The question is, will you let what loves you touch you, and will you be able to touch what it is you truly love?

What poetry will your life be in response to that gentle, kind, enduring, faithful and undying love?

And now here is my secret, a very simple secret; it is only with the heart that one can see rightly, what is essential is invisible to the eye.

Antoine de Saint-Exupery

In books of famous quotations, the name Antoine de Saint-Exupery appears frequently with his views, thoughts and wisdoms on many subjects to do with philosophy and the human condition. But who exactly was he, and in what way does his life experience frame and give context to the quotation that is the subject of this chapter?

As his name suggests he was born into an Aristocratic French family at the very beginning of the last century in 1900. At that time, being born into the upper echelons of French society meant that it was possible therefore to regards one's profession as being just that – an aristocrat. The benefits that came with title, privilege and social position dated back hundreds of years in his family to well before the French Revolution of the 18th century.

He was also a distinguished writer, poet and pioneering aviator and lost his life in the Second World War in 1944 whilst flying a reconnaissance mission around the Rhone valley gathering intelligence about German troop movements. He was only 44 when he died.

His most famous work is undoubtedly a novella called The Little Prince which was first published in 1943 a year before his death. The illustrations within the book are done by Antoine de Saint-Exupery himself and their simple, innocent beauty are an important part of the book's enduring appeal.

It tells the story of a young prince who somehow falls to Earth from an asteroid and there he meets a pilot. Many people obviously interpret the book as being an allegory of Antoine de Saint-Exupery's own life given that he himself was a pilot.

Having being translated into at least 250 languages and sold in excess of 140 million copies worldwide it is one of the biggest selling books of all time. Part of the reason for the success of the book is that whilst it is ostensibly a children's book, it has many themes within its content that reflect on human nature and therefore is equally as accessible for adults as it is for children.

Whilst written in a rather simplistic style, the book nevertheless contains powerful observations on philosophy, morality, social criticism and human relationships both with other humans and nature. It also speaks powerfully of how the adult world is different to the world of the child and because of what has been lost (due the loss of innocence by things becoming literally adulterated) that adults then seem to impose their perception of what is true and real on children and therefore cause them to lose this innocence and accordingly their very essence.

Children move from freely and naturally engaging with both the seen and unseen worlds equally and naturally to becoming much more focused (literally) on the seen world to such a degree that as they get older and become adults, not only can they no longer see this hidden world, but they cease to believe that it even or ever existed.

Adults often think that children and the world that they believe in, or think they live in, is sweet, innocent, naïve and full of imagination and fantasy where the lines between reality and fantasy sometimes get blurred with secret worlds of fairies, goblins, imaginary friends and magic. Yet compared to this world, the world of adults can only be seen as strange and peculiar in the extreme, especially when one sees how adults behave and what they do. Who then really is living in the world of fantasy, delusion and false truths?

Given the simple accessibility of the writing style and the ubiquity of the book it is therefore hardly surprising that many of his quotations appear in anthologies of sayings of famous people.

The quotation above is possibly the most famous of all his quotations and indeed is often the one used to describe the essence of what The Little Prince is ostensibly about. (These words are in fact spoken to the little prince in the book by a fox).

Another quotation that is often mentioned is:

"You become responsible, forever, for what you have tamed."

The appeal of the book is enduring and this is partly because of its style together with its multi-levelled meanings and moral. It really defies simply classification or putting into any kind of neat box. Is it for children or is it for adults? The point is that either set of eyes can read the book and see a message between the lines that is especially for them.

Is the glass half empty or half full? Yes!

It is clear which side the author is on, or at least which side has the better eyes. For the background to the little prince's visit to Earth is that before coming here he has in fact visited six other asteroids other than his home one and each one he found to be occupied by a foolish, selfish, narrow-minded, egotistical adult.

He then comes to Earth in the hope that things will be different here.

The book works, because it is written in a way that children in their reality understand well. This is the world of imagination rather than the world of strict realism and rationality mostly occupied by adults. Because it is written this way adults have to let go of their adult world "truth" because some of the things in the book clearly aren't logical or practical to the perceived reality of adults.

In other words, there has to be a letting go of the known and a willing suspension of disbelief before adults can gain access to the meaning of what is being written about and the truth of what is being written about can gain access to them.

Children on the other hand do not have suspend disbelief because they are much more in their natural state of imagination rather than clinical rationality.

One could say that in more modern neuroscience parlance that children are much more based in the right hemisphere of the brain which is to do with things like the imagination and the flux and flow of reality whereas adults are much more centred in left hemisphere influences of things being fixed, separate and physical where truth is linear and much more compartmentalised.

A large part of growing up and becoming educated is learning how to move from the truth of imagination to the truth of things being just things.

This education process could also be seen as a movement, not to the head as being the centre of primary importance, but rather one away from the heart. So we move away from what we feel to what we think.

De Saint-Exupery's countryman Descartes and his *"I think therefore I am"* has a lot to answer for!

Turning now to the quote itself, there is clearly an appeal and a challenge within it that faces the person reading it with a choice which is a bit like the challenge within optical illusion pictures where what one sees in the picture depends on the way one looks at it.

For example, is the following picture of a rabbit or a duck?

It obviously depends on which way one looks at it and which side of the brain is doing the looking. What is interesting however is that it is not possible to see both the duck and the rabbit at the same time and that in order to see one then the observer must let go of the view of the other.

This is why adults don't see the world as children see it, because they can't and won't let go of their view of the world which is one of the hard reality of the visible.

Another example of seeing different things in the same picture is below:

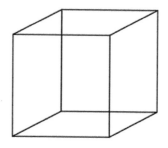

Look at the cube and decide whether or not spatially in three dimensions through the two dimensions of the page, it looks as though, on first impression, the cube proceeds from bottom left to top right or from top right down to bottom left.

If on first impression the cube looks as though it proceeds from left bottom to top right, then you are in all likelihood an adult! Or at least more placed in the left hemisphere of the brain which is the one we spend more and more time in as we become adults.

If you see the top right down to the bottom left version of the cube first, then you are more likely to be a child or occupying the right hemisphere of the brain which is the one we spend more time in as children until we begin that awful disease of "growing up" that adults force us to do!

Having seen the cube proceeding from direction or the other can you then see it proceeding in the other direction than your first impression?

And equally importantly, can you feel some kind of shift going on in your head / brain as you do so?

One thing is clear, and that is in order to see the cube going the other way one has to let go of the belief that it only proceeds in one direction.

Truth depends on the observer and:

    a. What one is looking to find and
    b. What we have trained our eyes to see.

What is visible isn't necessarily the only thing that it is possible to see. Witness testimonies of the same event bear this out with often there being apparently opposite yet honest opinions of the actual events that occurred.

Therefore, there is not only the visible but the invisible that De Saint-Exupery speaks of.

Just because something is invisible to our eyes doesn't mean that it isn't there, it just means what it literally says in that it is not visible. This is clearly so in that some animals can see things that outside the range of our visibility in the ultraviolet and infrared ends of the spectrum, and others can hear things that are outside our hearing range.

Because we don't see something doesn't mean it isn't there. (And on the other side of the coin just because we think that something is there doesn't mean that it is!)

The word invisible means that something is there, but we simply can't see it. Just like some people simply cannot see that the cube can also be perceived from the other way that their first impression tells them it does.

What De Saint-Exupery seems to be telling us is that yes there are the eyes that link to our brains but there are also "eyes" that are of the heart. These are the eyes of feelings, emotions, imagination and so on.

It is often said that the eyes are the window to the soul. But they can only be a window to the soul if they are in fact truly open. Otherwise if the window to and out from the soul is shut then the eyes of the brain take over and we only see what our adult eyes allow us to see.

What is essential is invisible to the eye.

This suggests that without the eyes of the heart the essence of what something truly is in its being and in its truth cannot be seen.

It might therefore be interesting to take a look in the mirror sometime and consider which eyes are doing the looking and what the different eyes see looking back. The you of the eyes of the brain or the you of the eyes of the heart?

Just who or what is it that you are looking at? And who or what is it that is looking back?

While you are proclaiming peace with your lips, be careful to have it even more fully in your heart.

Francis of Assisi

Saint Francis of Assisi was born around 1181 and died in 1226 aged around only 44 years old. He was born in Assisi to Italian parents and whilst baptised Giovanni he was called Francesco (meaning "the Frenchman") by his father possibly in recognition of the fact that Francis was born whilst he father was away in France on business, or perhaps because his father loved France and all things French. Whatever the reason, the name of endearment stuck and so today the world remembers not Giovanni of Assisi but Francis.

Francis was born into a well to do family and it is known that his mother was a noblewoman and his father may have been a merchant or trader or similar. So even though Francis came from a large family of seven children they wanted for nothing and lived a rather privileged and carefree life.

However, despite this life of privilege it seems that Francis had a natural inclination towards justice and charity for the story is recounted about when he was young he worked on his father's market stall selling cloth and velvet and one day a beggar came up to Francis on the stall and asked Francis for alms or charity. It is said that at the end of the day Francis went after the beggar and having caught up with him gave the beggar everything that he had in his pockets. For doing this he was chided and mocked by his friends and his father when he found out flew into a rage with Francis about the stupidity of his actions.

Whatever the truth of that particular story it seems that Francis's life became a journey that caused him to renounce his life of luxury and privilege and follow what he believed to be the true example of the life of Jesus Christ and the message about his life contained within the gospels.

In particular, it seems that Francis fully embraced the message of poverty preached by Jesus and he came increasingly to believe that the true wealth of living was not to be found in this world through material goods, but in the richness of the spiritual world and the next world after this one. He profoundly believed the teaching that it is harder for a rich man to enter the kingdom of heaven that for a camel to pass through the eye of a needle.

This separating himself from materialism was probably a gradual process although it is quite possible that a serious illness he suffered in 1204 and the mystical experiences he had at that time expedited this "conversion" to the way of truth and poverty. It certainly led to increased clashes with his father, who not only chided him but also beat him for giving away the profits of the business that his father had worked so hard to build up. In the end Francis publicly renounced his father and gave away all his remaining wordly goods and assumed the life of a beggar and an ascetic.

It is then said that in 1209 Francis heard a sermon based around Matthew Chapter 10 verse 9 that changed his life forever. This verse is where Jesus tells his disciples that the kingdom of heaven is upon them and that they should go forth without money, a walking-stick or even shoes for the road.

Francis took this message literally and deeply to heart and embraced the life of having absolutely nothing and living the life of charity to its fullest and most basic. He then began to preach his message of repentance and that people should follow the teachings of Jesus to the utmost and most literal meaning for therein lay – the way and the truth and the light.

Also around this time, when he had about 11 followers, he journeyed with them to Rome to seek the permission of Pope Innocent III to establish a new religious order based on these simple principles. Whilst the pope was initially sceptical about the idea, it is said that he had a dream in which he saw Francis holding up the Basilica of St John Lateran i.e. the church that pre-dated the Basilica of St Peter, and he saw this as a sign. He therefore decided to grant consent to this very small band of devoted men to establish their own order known then as the "Fratres Minores" or Little Brothers.

With this official blessing from the pope and its simple message the Order became popular as its message spread throughout Italy and new recruits sought to join. Around 1211 it is said that Clare of Assisi heard Francis preach his message and she was deeply touched by its simplicity and integrity and consequently she set up her own order known as The Poor Clares, with both Orders still existing to this day.

Francis has been venerated down the ages for his deep love of nature and all God's creatures. He believed that it was within the gift, and was also the duty, of all creatures to praise God and that human beings had an obligation to protect and enjoy nature as both the stewards of God's creation and as creatures ourselves. In this Francis believed that we need to treat all creatures with the same reverence and love and fully embraced the view that one should *"treat others as you yourself would wish to be treated"*. This didn't just apply to other people, but to all creatures and nature itself.

So renowned is Francis for his love and reverence of nature that in 1979 the then pope made Francis the patron saint of ecology.

Francis had a profound influence during his lifetime and his simple message resonated with many who saw the institution of the Church and its pomp and bureaucracy as having become out of touch with the core message and values as preached and demonstrated by Jesus.

Francis tapped into this feeling and his message was in its own way a *"back to basics"* realignment towards living a truly religious life.

There are many stories about Saint Francis and his genuine piety, devotion, simplicity and his relationship with nature. Some of these stories are probably apocryphal but even so they do reflect his genuine endearment and respect for nature, creation and the works of God.

In one sense therefore he can be seen as a pioneer of the modern day environmental and ecology movements having preceded them by the fact of a mere 800 years! He certainly might be accused by some modern day scientists as being naïve and New Age in his thinking but given that he lived 800 years ago he can hardly be accused as being New Age!

He was in fact a holist in that he saw everything in Creation as being inter-connected and inter-dependent and that everything needed to be treated with reverence and respect. In this he anticipated the current scientific concept of the butterfly wing effect in that each and every action on the planet affects each and every other organism.

Whatever one thinks of Francis and however modern revisionism might want to try and explain away his radical and fundamental views through him possibly suffering some condition or other, one thing is however clear and that is that Francis *"walked the walk"* of what he taught and preached. One could never say that he was the kind of preacher who said *"Do as I say and not as I do"*. And either consciously or unconsciously he saw or anticipated the need for the Church to embody and live the message of the teachings of Jesus and not just preach it.

This is evidenced by the fact that he travelled to the Middle East and sought to make a peace with the Muslim world after the terrible wars and violence of the Crusades. It must be a testament to his genuineness that after the Crusades it was only the Franciscans who were allowed to remain in the Holy land as true custodians of the message of Christianity. This was partially no doubt due to the fact that they preached non-violence and as such posed no physical threat. In this Francis again preceded Ghandi and his message of non-violence by a factor of 800 years.

This idea of a truly religious life being one that is actually lived rather than is assumed through intellectual knowledge is a very powerful one. For it goes beyond the popular saying:

"As a bird is known by its song, so is a man by his words."

Words are easy to say but Francis was all about action because to him, to say one thing and do another was nothing other than hypocrisy.

This is reminiscent of the exchange in Pilgrim's Progress when Faithful (a friend of the Pilgrim Christian) whilst on the journey with Christian meets someone called Talkative who regales Faithful with much talk about great and noble truths. Yet when probed by Faithful at the instigation of Christian, Talkative is found to have a huge gap between what he "knows" and preaches and how he lives his actual life.

Having spent some time with Talkative and being greatly impressed by him when quizzed by Christian, Faithful starts to wonder if he has been deceived by Talkative and asks Christian whether this is the case.

To which Christian replies:

"Remember the proverb: They say and do not: but the Kingdom of God is not in word, but in power. He (Talkative) talketh of prayer, of repentance, of faith and of the new birth, but he knows but only to talk of them. I have been in his family, and have observed him both at home and at abroad; and I know what I say of him is of truth. His house is as empty of religion, as the white of an egg is as empty of savour. There is neither prayer nor sign of repentance for sin; yes, the brute in his kind serves God better than he."

Gradually Faithful begins to see the point that Christian is making to him about that part of the human condition that Christian is highlighting to do with inconsistency and Faithful articulates this as follows:

"Well I see that saying and doing are two things, and hereafter I shall better observe this distinction."

Faithful then confronts Talkative about his inconsistency and when confronted Talkative withdraws from his engagement without Faithful and accuses Faithful of not being "fit to be discoursed with."

Christian then reflects on Faithful's exchange with Talkative and summates it as follows:

"How Talkative at first lifts up his plumes!
How bravely doth he speak! How he presumes
To drive down all before him! But so soon
As Faithful talks of heart-work, like the Moon
That's past the full, into the wane he goes;
And so will all, but he that heart-work knows."

This is quite a remarkable passage for it speaks of work not done by the mind and intellect, but of work done by and from the heart. Particularly since modern science is starting to discover that the heart isn't merely an organ that pumps blood around the body but that it has its own form of intelligence, memory and resonance. For example, people who have had heart transplants have discovered that after having had their transplant they have developed tastes, cravings, attitudes and even behaviours of the donors of the transplanted organs even though they didn't know either the donor or anything about their life.

This phenomenon is called organ memory syndrome, and science through what is called *"cell memory theory"* confirms that there is no reason why this cannot be the actual case.

This has been documented in research and one example is as follows:

Claire Sylvia, a heart transplant recipient who received the organ from an 18-year-old male who died in a motorcycle accident, reported having a craving for beer and chicken nuggets after the surgery. The heart transplant recipient also began to have reoccurring dreams about a man named 'Tim L'. Upon searching the obituaries, Sylvia found out her donor's name was in fact Tim and that he loved all of the food that she now craved.

Defoe knew about the heart being integral to the integrity of the person as much what they knew and what came out of their mouth.

And from the quotation at the start of this chapter we can see that Francis was saying exactly the same thing that Christian was saying to Faithful 450 years later.

In our modern language we might say that one needs to be wary of spin doctors and those who weave different truths and realities. Francis cuts through all this pretence and says that you can't fool the heart.

It may be possible to fool some of the people all of the time, and all of the people some of the time but you can't fool all of the people all of the time. But perhaps it is not possible to fool the heart at all unless the head gets in the way? For the heart knows, not just because it knows what it knows, but it knows what it feels.

We experience this frequently in modern times when public figures are exposed as being inconsistent or hypocrites for preaching or moralising about issues and then being found out as being "guilty" themselves. Then there follows the public apology about how they have let down their family, their friends, the people who trusted them and God and then they seek forgiveness.

Of course they are not really sorry at all really. They are only sorry that they got caught out. Much like Talkative was sorry when Faithful finally saw through his "act".

Whatever our 21st century eyes and ears may think of Francis and his life and message eight centuries later, surely there is a message from his life that can still resonate for us all today in that it says, live a simple, throughout, consistent and genuine life that is full of reverence, respect, gratitude and value. Do not exploit any of the works or other lives in Creation because they do not belong to you and they have their own rights and covenant with their Creator as you do.

Love all things and cherish them as you yourself would want to be loved and cherished.

Such a creed might not solve all the problems of the world but then again it just might be that many of them could magically disappear.

It is said that 1% of the world's population now owns 50% of the world's wealth. But are they truly the world's richest people?

For maybe Francis had something that all the material wealth in the world can't buy?

And what was that?

Well perhaps it was the fact that Francis found the place in himself where he was happy to have nothing and thereby nothing had him?

And thus he was free.

The Divine Spirit does not reside in any except the joyful heart.

The Talmud

The Talmud is the book of Rabbinic Judaism and was and is meant to be a guide to some of the central tenets of Judaism both for Rabbis and the Jewish people themselves. It is primarily a book of scholarship based on the study and the interpretation of books like the Torah and how their key principles should be applied in everyday life. Originally it was passed on by way of oral tradition, and it was only much later that there was perceived to be a need for all these interpretations to be gathered in some kind of written form.

Perhaps this is just as well for when written down the cumulated text runs to something in the order of 6,200 pages. That's quite a lot to commit to memory so probably it was just as well that it should be written down!

The Talmud contains the teachings and opinions of many rabbis collected over a long period of time on a whole variety of subjects from ethics to philosophy to Jewish practice to customs and lore to history and many other matters. It therefore forms the basis of Jewish law and its code of practice.

The Talmud is not a doctrinal book in that it is not regarded as being a dogma or indeed the word of God. It is in fact a temporal book in that it contains the views of human beings i.e. rabbis and their understandings, beliefs and opinions on how the sacred books of the

Jewish faith such as the Torah should be interpreted and applied in practice.

Some of the opinions and views expressed in the Talmud may diverge, disagree or offer different interpretations, not only of the sacred scripture but also on history, custom and practice, tradition and so on. Hence the extremely lively debates and arguments over such matters of faith and practice within the Jewish community, because not only are there the sacred scriptures to interpret and apply, but there are also the interpretations of countless rabbis to be argued over as well!

Originally the Torah wasn't written down either and so without a tradition of written scripture to rely on the Jewish faith developed its roots from the oral tradition of rabbis discoursing their views and discussing them in public. This led not only to very lively debate as to the meaning of God, religion and faith and what it meant to be a good Jew, but also meant that Judaism developed more than one type of belief and structure and thus various schools of Judaism developed over the centuries.

Many still exist today with everything from ultra conservative, to very liberal interpretations that seek to bring Judaism into the 21st century, to some forms that seek to separate the secular and religious aspects of Judaism completely.

It is therefore not only impossible but also rather lazy to try and bottom line Judaism as being boxed into a simplistic definition that fits into a box when it clearly doesn't. Especially when one of the books of interpretation that tries to act as kind of teaching guide for how to be a good Jew runs to over 6,000 pages and contains a multitude of different opinions as to address the major issues of theology and philosophy to the minutiae of every day, mundane tasks.

It certainly isn't meant to be a book of answers, but rather is a book of opinions, and up until the time it was collected into a written down form any valid opinion that had been collected was included, though exactly what constituted a valid opinion is not entirely clear.

It is also not entirely clear exactly when the Talmud was reduced to its written form, and although the first written copy dates from 1342 it is likely that there were written versions some time before that. The oral tradition goes back even further than that.

What can be said is that there are probably as many versions of the Talmud and its interpretation as there are versions of the Christian Bible.

Even the status of the Talmud itself is disputed with many conservative and fundamentalist branches of Judaism regarding it is being authoritative and binding, whilst neo-liberal Jews say that it isn't binding as it is the work of man, not God. Therefore, it should only be regarded as being for advisory purposes alone.

This difference of views is probably to be expected, as it reflects the difference of views expressed within the Talmud itself, both as to the subject matter the various entries relate to and also the status that those making their statements regard their own entries as having. For some regard what they say as being the truth and dogma, whereas others seem to be clear that they are only expressing an opinion or even simply a philosophical point or perhaps a sentiment.

It is doubtful that one is expected to know yet alone follow what is said in each and every entry. Otherwise this could lead to the very inconvenient circumstance of having to carry a 6000 plus page book everywhere so it can be consulted in every situation where one doesn't know what to do or how to respond.

It seems therefore that a common sense approach to the Talmud is needed and that whilst it is meant as guidance and assistance it is also a healthy forum for debate and argue stretch.

Although having said that many of the entries are simple, practical, useful, helpful, constructive, wise and non-controversial.

It seems that many of the entries come from the experience of rabbis who probably lived long lives and witnessed many things about life, the lessons it teaches, and the locations and understandings that are needed in order to live a clean, decent and moral life. The fact that this relates to a person of the Jewish faith and creed is obvious, but the thoughts, ideas and views expressed in it can also in many circumstances be regarded as being applicable to the human race generally.

There is no reason why a non-Jewish person can't read the Talmud and find useful advice and counsel and find some useful advice, tips, signposts, understandings and wisdoms that they too can apply into and out from their life. And no doubt there may be entries that they will not wish follow as well.

So with that in mind as context it is time to look at the quote from the Talmud that forms the title of this chapter.

The Divine Spirit does not reside in any except the joyful heart.

This is a very powerful statement or assertion, and is certainly not one that can be subjected to any kind of scientific or empirical testing.

For how can one devise an experiment to definitively prove one way or the other that the Divine Spirit does or doesn't exist? Or how can one test to find out whether a heart can be joyful or not? It is possible to test as to whether it is healthy or the heartbeat is irregular, but as of writing there is no known instrument that can test as to whether the heart contains joy or not.

Yet many cultures on many continents all seem to identify the heart as being much, much more that simply an organ that pumps the blood around the body. It is also seen by most of these cultures as being linked to very powerful emotions like love, joy and happiness. It is also often regarded as being a precious home within the person for all that they love, cherish and hold dear.

It is seen as being very important in the role of religious devotion and connection and is an important bridge between the affairs of God and the affairs of the human.

What this entry seems to be saying is that there is indeed a sacred part to the experience of being human and that this sacred signal originates from somewhere else. Or perhaps it is everywhere in that it is omnipresent? It cannot be possessed or owned and that all one can do is to create a home within oneself where it can happily abide and dwell within the person.

The second part of the entry suggests that a condition precedent exists for this divine influence to reside within the person and this is that the person have joy in their heart.

This raises the question, how can joy live within a person's heart?
It also asks - what exactly is joy and what are its essential features?

Are these scientific questions, philosophical ones or perhaps moral or religious ones or perhaps a combination of all of these?

It certainly seems that science and medical approaches to these questions haven't yet been able to develop a test to determine whether a heart can be joyful and if it can whether the Divine Spirit can therefor live in it.

What is clear is that a reductionist, materialist approach isn't going to provide an empirical proof that the Divine Spirit is made of the stuff that can be analysed in the way that perhaps the chemical constituents of a liquid or solid can be.

Yet many cultures carry the idea that the heart is the home of many passions and emotions such as love, hope and joy and how important it is to make one's heart a home for all that is good, valued, cherished and loved and not to make it a home for negativity.

This has been known for countless centuries and well pre-dates what we think are relatively modern concepts such as the influence of mind over matter and the placebo effect.

If you think the worst, you attract the worst.

If you think the best, you hold the best.
If you see what is wrong in things or other people, then it is what is wrong in you that is doing the looking.
If you see the good in things and other people, then it is much more likely that they will likewise see the good in you.

In other words, we become tuning forks for what resonates in us as being important. Or put another way be become like what we like. And importantly we also become like what we don't like. So the warning in this is be careful what you don't like and how much and how often you don't like it. For the more you become pre-occupied with what you don't like the less space there is in you for what you do like because you have become literally pre...occupied by negative things.

As they say, birds of a feather flock together, or fine goes to fine and coarse goes to coarse.

This further suggests that there is a twinning and mutuality in the relationship between the Divine Spirit and having a joyful heart. This has to be important for it indicates that a pre-requisite for creating space in one's heart for the Divine Spirit to reside in is that one must feel joy. It doesn't suggest that one should feel guilt, fear, shame, unworthy or that one is a sinner or that God (whatever one perceives that to be) is an angry or punishing God.

This is extremely powerful, for it goes against most orthodox and classic religious teaching that suggests that we humans have "fallen" and that we are somehow lesser, unworthy and need to repent and seek forgiveness for this state of affairs.

Yet whilst we may have all done things that are indeed lesser or unworthy of our design and pedigree, this suggests that the higher response to the gift of life and being is that we respond with joy to the marvel and miracle that life truly is.

Just like we all know the feeling of being at lesser and how that shrinks and diminishes us, we also know that the feelings of things like happiness and joy expand us and fill us up with gratitude, hope, warmth and kindness and perhaps most importantly of all value and respect.

One cannot have a true value and respect for walking through a wilderness forest or perhaps an oasis in the desert whilst at the same time thinking about turning that view into a logging venture or a water bottling plant.

Yet we often do this to ourselves and each other by what we think and what do and most importantly of all by what we perceive.

What we perceive determines what we receive.

Yet none of this really answers our questions as to what is divine and what is joy?

They enigmatically defy definition and perhaps thankfully so. Because if we define them then that suggest we take the fineness out of them and therefore also ourselves.

But having said that, a short visit to the dictionary suggest some starter ways to perhaps think about these qualities or states?

Divine – Of God, of supreme excellence and worth. To perceive or understand something by intuition or insight.

Joy – Happiness, pleasure, contentment, delight.

This suggests that there are other systems in us that can know things without or even before rational thought or proof can be found. Rocket science might be able to find other planets but it can't find joy or love.

We find love with another when we find it in ourselves and we receive it when we give it.

Surely it is the same with the Divine Spirit and joy?

We find it in God and Creation when we find it in ourselves and in each other.

Joy might not solve some of the problems of the world, but neither on the other hand can the problems of the world create more joy.

What might be the case however is that if all have a little more joy in their hearts then we might just find divine inspiration in finding new, kind, compassionate and loving ways that would help alleviate many of the problems the world faces and perhaps we can even cause some of them to magically disappear.

The Talmud seems to have some eminently sound and sage advice for us all in this regard regardless of our religion, faith, race or creed. A joyful heart doesn't discriminate or judge on such terms or any for that matter.

It is said that to err is human and to forgive is divine.

Perhaps therefore to have a heart full of joy is not only also divine but it doesn't feel like an error either!

An artist needn't be a clergyman or a churchwarden, but he certainly must have a warm heart for his fellow men.

Vincent Van Gogh

Perhaps you didn't know this, but Vincent Van Gogh was born under the astrological star sign of Aries for he was born on 30th March 1853.

Whether one believes in astrology or not it is rather interesting to say the least that Vincent certainly fits many of the so called archetypal features that one might typically place with an Aries person.

Passionate, impulsive, headstrong, fiery, intense, always starting things but not always finishing them, driven, singular, original, emotional, headstrong, compulsive, unyielding, flamboyant and more. Vincent embodied so many of these characteristics in his short but very intense and productive life.

I first became aware of Vincent and his work when I heard the song Vincent on the album American Pie by Don Maclean which was released in the early 1970's. I was a massive fan of the song American Pie and with my friends we all learned the lyrics of the song off by heart and sang them relentlessly as we dreamed the American Dream in New Zealand and wondered whether the lyrics were about Buddy Holly and "the day the music had died" some 13 years earlier in 1959.

Don Maclean was not only the writer and singer of a very cool song, but he was also a very cool guy because he refused to talk about what the song was actually about.

Was it about Elvis Presley when he talks about the Jester who sang for the king and queen in a coat he borrowed from James Dean? Or perhaps John Lennon? Nobody knew, but what we did know is that the song was simply irresistible as we belted it out together when we heard it on the radio.

And how could anyone not love lyrics like:

> Did you write the Book of Love?
> And do you have faith in God above,
> If the Bible tells you so.
> Do you believe in rock n roll?
> Can music save your mortal soul?
> And can you teach me how to dance real slow?

We really felt free singing along with the song, and it was as much about the feeling from the song as the lyrics. The release of the song somehow hit a chord literally that touched many hearts and many lives in that era.

Perhaps it is no wonder therefore that it was rumoured that Don Maclean himself was supposedly the inspiration for the song also released around that time by Roberta Flack called Killing Me Softly with his Song.

We didn't care whether it was true or not. We simply loved the message from the song that somehow we felt was for us and was with us in ways we didn't really understand or need to understand.

Notwithstanding the lyrics of the song talking about the day the music died, it clearly didn't and hadn't died because Don was keeping it alive big time.

On the back of hearing American Pie, I thought that the rest of the album must be as totally amazing as that song and so I bought it with my hard earned pocket money and it was one of the first albums I ever bought.

And on the album was this other song called Vincent, about someone I had never heard of; Vincent van Gogh, a Dutch painter who lived in the 19th century apparently.

With the incredible success of the single American Pie this meant that Don Maclean's follow up song was going to get plenty of airplay on the radio, and the song that was the follow up single was in fact Vincent. And what a different song it proved to be, in tempo at least, if perhaps not in sentiment.

Yet it was in its own way equally wonderful.

Somehow the lyrics captured something that conveyed to the world some of the feelings, passions and frequencies that Vincent had captured in his wild and free paintings. Yet the song did so in such a quiet, intimate, profound, moving and beautiful way.

It is not an exaggeration to say that with this song Don Maclean brought into consciousness in a substantial way a greater awareness of the fact of Vincent's life and his incredible body of work. Suddenly the demand for Vincent's work skyrocketed, and from his paintings not being worth that very much he became the most sought after artist in the world. His painting Sunflowers was bought for tens of millions of dollars making it the most expensive painting in the world at that time.

Vincent only ever sold one painting during the course of his short, turbulent, passionate life. How ironic this is considering what his art came to be worth 100 years later. The fact that he himself couldn't sell his paintings clearly shows that he didn't paint to court popularity, nor did he compromise no matter how much his brother Theo tried to help him and advise him to make better use of his clearly prodigious talent.

When I heard this song by Don Maclean I became very interested in finding out who this Vincent was and given that it was on the radio so often it didn't take long to hear some stories being told by the DJs that it was about Vincent van Gogh a Post—Impressionist painter, whatever that meant.

I therefore went into a bookshop in my home town of Christchurch, New Zealand and looked around for a book that might have some pictures and found one called The Impressionists which was very large book indeed with chapters about the various Impressionist painters such as Monet, Degas, Manet, Renoir, Seurat, van Gogh and others plus lots of colour pictures of their work.

It was a lovely book, but very expensive for a teenage schoolboy so I didn't know if I could afford to buy it. But then it was mother's birthday coming up and so I shamelessly and rather selfishly bought it for her as her birthday present whilst not letting on that really I had bought it as much, if not more, for me instead of her.

However, luckily for me, my mother was quite an artistic person in her own way and she really liked the book and it kept pride of place as one of those coffee table picture books people like to have to show that they like art. So it sat there for years with guests occasionally picking it up and seeing on the inside cover that I had bought it for my mother as her birthday present. Perhaps this impressed visitors into thinking that I was as impressive a person as perhaps the Impressionists were impressive painters?

Sadly, I don't think was quite the case due to my motives, but I loved the book and so did my mother so who needs to know otherwise?

When I read the book and saw the pictures and especially those by Vincent, including the one called Starry, Starry Night in the first line of Don Maclean's song it took my breath away. I then really "got" what Don Maclean was singing about.

Such boldness, such vivacity, such beauty, such originality, such an "other worldliness" about it, a presence, a spiritual something that couldn't be explained. I was transfixed, mesmerised and hypnotised by his work. I didn't understand it at one level, but at another level I knew that something spoke to something in me from somewhere beyond language and explanation. It was almost too beautiful to the point of being painful.

No wonder Don Maclean put the line in his song:

"But 1 could have told you Vincent, this world was never meant for one as beautiful as you."

As I learned more about Vincent's life and how tragic it was it many ways so I learned more about his art, his life and the meaning and power within Don Maclean's song and so I loved it even more.

Curiously enough, about 8 years later having now finished school and University I found myself living in London and working in central London as a bicycle messenger (before the invention of the Internet) delivering letters and parcels in and around all the wondrous sights and galleries there were to see there.

One of my favourite things to do when I had a few minutes between deliveries was to go into the National Gallery, which was free to enter, in my shorts and sandals and T shirt with my message bleeper on my bag and go and look at the countless pictures in there. My favourite section was the Impressionists, and particularly Vincent's work.

Seeing these original pictures was simply astonishing. For rather than being flat on the canvas as I had thought they were originally (I must have thought they were watercolours or similar) they were in fact painted in oils, and in van Gogh's hand they leapt off the canvas and were nearly three dimensional such was the depth of oil paint that he used on his pictures.

No wonder he kept asking his brother Theo to send him more money so he could buy more paint!

The first time I saw his pictures I just stood there with my mouth open, amazed and incredulous at how daring and truly original his work was.

I spent many a happy hour in there gazing in a semi-meditative state at this heroic and colossal attempt by Vincent to capture both the form and essence of the subject matter before him.

He may have been part of what is now called The Impressionist School but what he painted wasn't taught in any school as far as I could tell, and nor did he seem to be within a movement of any kind other than what moved him and what he was moved by.

As another coincidence, some time later I later worked in Isleworth, West London and just around the corner from where I worked was a blue plaque on the outside of a house there that stated that Vincent had lived there for a short time on a visit there in the 1870's.

I often walked past it and wondered what he was like and how I would have wanted to meet him somehow from the future and tell him how much his work was now loved, respected and valued, and hope that perhaps that knowledge from the future may have eased his pain of so being in the present that he literally couldn't handle it.

Suffering for one's art took on an entirely different meaning where Vincent's art was concerned for almost everyone knows the story of how he cut off his ear, or at least a large part of it and sent it to a prostitute.

Vincent had great difficulty in walking that tightrope between genius and madness, between the mundane and ordinary and the sublime and the magnificent, the everyday and the almighty, the assumed and the transcendent.

He knew that truth didn't depend on a name, a title, a qualification or a role.

Truth for Vincent was a state and that state was the art of the art of what it means to be truly alive.

To be truly alive to the art of the life within a person needed to have a warm heart not a cold one.

Being a clergyman or a churchwarden guaranteed nothing, for in the absence of something higher and deeper and present within the person it was just another job like every other job.

What makes the difference is what lives within us, what we love, what we care about and how we care and express that love for all things.

That is the true art of the artist.

Not that one has to be able to use a paintbrush, but that somehow a person finds within themselves the ability to be able to be moved by the nature within us all and the nature than sustains us all. The nature of nature herself in all her beauty that makes her so truly magnificent, and the nature of true human nature that makes us who and what we truly are as human beings.

The art of being moved by great and powerful things.

Truth lives in the grace and the grant of all that is host and hosanna to our experience here on Earth.

A hard place to live in, and a harder place to leave.

So yes this world was never meant for someone as beautiful as Vincent.

But then again it was.

For Vincent opened the door to greater perception for us all to each find our unique truth as to what makes our hearts warm to all that is great and good.

And what is that heart the door towards?

That Starry, Starry Night within each and every one of us.

There is no charm equal to tenderness of the heart.

Jane Austen

Jane Austen was an English novelist who was born in 1775 and died in 1817 at the relatively young age of 41 from an illness that may have been a cancer or possibly even a form of tuberculosis. She came from a very well off, close knit family and although she herself never married she wrote mainly romantic novels about affairs of the heart set mainly among the upper classes and landed gentry from which she herself came.

She wrote some of the most well-known novels of all time, with works such as Pride and Prejudice, Sense and Sensibility, Emma, Northanger Abbey and Mansfield Park. Many of her works have been adapted both for television and the cinema and often on more than one occasion. It is rare that many years go by without there being some new adaptation of her works being produced.

Yet despite their fame today, her works were not well-known in her own lifetime and nor were they that positively reviewed at the time. Indeed, most people didn't know that Jane herself was the author of these great works because she initially published them anonymously.

But because of their subject matter and context i.e. being set amongst the upper classes, they soon grew in popularity, firstly among those classes themselves and in time among the population generally.

Today critics take mixed views of the merit of Jane's work, with everything from radical feminists either loving or hating her work, with Jane being regarded as either being an early pioneer of championing the role and merits of women, to others saying that she in fact entrenched the role of women as being subservient, weak, emotional and governed far too much by affairs of the heart rather than the head. Other critics say that her work is at best lightweight and somewhat trivial and lacks depth and substance and that her style can at times be twee and giddy.

However, what the critics can't argue with is the enduring popularity of Jane's works through many different changes in our societies since the time when the novels were written just over 200 years ago. Given that our modern world today would be mostly unrecognisable to Jane, she must have therefore captured themes, morals and behaviours that comment and reflect upon the human condition in how we relate and how we conduct our relationships.

Part of her skill was in being able to write about a completely different world from the one that most people lived in, and yet in a way that the reader could still recognise themes and qualities expressed in her books, both in themselves and in others they knew.

The above picture of Jane drawn by her beloved sister and closest friend Cassandra appears to show Jane to be a somewhat simple and plain girl despite her pedigree and upbringing. It fails to reveal her clever, witty and insightful awareness into the complex world of human relationships, love, betrayal and redemption.

But maybe there is something in those eyes that are seeing much more than they are letting on?

It certainly seems that Jane in her own life loved simple pleasures, but was by no means immune to some of the aspects that she wrote about through the lives of her characters.

Perhaps Jane played out some of her own feelings, longings and desires through the rich tapestry of the roller coater lives of her characters and the plots and twists and turns their lives became embroiled in?

Emma

Before she wrote this novel Jane said that: *"I am going to take a heroine whom no one but me will much like."*

Perhaps that is why she chose the name Emma for the lead character because the name Emma is Am Me backwards? Given that Jane's own personal circumstances mirrored those of Emma in some ways, in that both were affluent and single, perhaps some of Jane's personalty, both real and imagined, is played out through the life of her serial match-making heroine Emma? Although it seems that Jane herself didn't attempt to matchmake in the way that Emma almost addictively is driven to do. Maybe she longed to do so?

One also wonders whether Jane was aware and consciously employed the fact that the name Emma means Universal? Was Jane trying to say that some of the themes within her novel were indeed Universal and that the battle to find oneself, be happy and attain fulfillment lies in the struggle between the highly personal and local world of class, romance and marriage and the impersonal but vital worlds or things like, love, honour, virtue and loyalty?

One doesn't know, but certainly Jane was an astute writer on the subtleties of human emotions and feelings, and the machimations and games people play to get what they want and find who and what they need in order to be happy.

Sense and Sensibility

It is interesting also that one of her other great novels was Sense and Sensibility. This was written well over

100 years before the birth of modern neuro-science which revealed that we have two sides of the brain which have very different natures and takes on reality and how we perceive it. The left side is more to do with structure, order, planning, logic, form and systems, whereas the right side is much more to do with feelings, imagination, context, process, being and freedom.

Or in other words, there is probabaly no better way to describe their natures and their processes as being left side = sense and the right side = sensibility.

Perhaps purely by instinct or maybe more, Jane captured the tensions between these two natures within her title, and the whole book is an account of this great struggle between what one should do and what one is moved to do. We often charaterise this as being a battle between heart and head and it is, but it is also a clash between the priorities and focuses of the left and right sides of the brain.

Whereas the overall tendency of modern science is to look at these two natures of the left and right side of the brain from more of a left side of the brain focus i.e. from an analytical, reductionist, atomistic and materialistic standpoint, the greater power, passion and potency in fact lies in the right side of the brain because this is where things like ideas, beliefs, hopes and love come from.

It is this side of the brain that charms and is charmed by things and people.

This is why Jane states that: *"There is no charm that is greater than the tenderness of the heart."*

When we speak of the word charm it has more than one meaning for the superficial meaning indicates that one finds something to be warming, attractive, alluring and even cute or nice.

But at a deeper level when someone is charmed by something it can mean that someone or something has cast a spell over them and it can even indicate that there is some kind of magic or intoxication of the feelings that has been caused by another person.

Hence we often have the expression today that someone has engaged in a charm offensive in that they have tried to win another person over to a particular view or to enter into some kind of relationship to suit the needs of the charmer.

When we say that someone is a "charmer" it usually applies to men and we don't usually say it in a way that indicates that a person who is a charmer is a pleasant person. Rather, it suggests that they are manipulative and calculating. Somewhat like the character played by Bill Murray in the film Groundhog Day who tries to charm the character played by Andie MacDowell into sleeping with him.

Jane's novels do contain characters who indulge in this kind of "charming" or scheming, and Emma herself is a classic example of someone who is doing this herself for various reasons some of which are seemingly altruistic and others which are manipulative and controlling.

But what Jane seems to be alluding to in the quotation is the power of true and genuine feelings that come from the heart or the core of our being.

The dictionary uses words like delight, please, win over, appeal to, attract, captivate, allure, lure, dazzle, fascinate, bewitch, beguile, enchant, enthral, enrapture, enamour, seduce, mesmerise, hypnotise, spellbind, rivet, transfix, rapture, grip and enrapture as possible synonyms for the word charm which just goes to show how powerful a word it is.

Given therefore that charm can be used by either side of the brain towards either control of another for selfish means, or for genuine feelings of love and affection and care, it seems that the thing that makes the difference is the tenderness of the heart.

It is no coincidence therefore that in Jane's time, and still to an extent today, people would say that they tender their feelings and affections towards another.

A Tender is also seen in other contexts as being an offer towards the possibility of entering some kind of contractual relationship, whether that be an offer of services for hire or to tendering one's hand to another as an offer to become engaged to be married.

The high end of the words charm and tender are to do with holding and celebrating the best of another, and offering to share with that other person the best of oneself from the present onwards into a collaborative and mutually rewarding enterprise be it a contract or a marriage.

So what gets in the way of these tender feelings that live in and belong with the heart? What prevents the natural flow of feelings both within the person themselves, and also towards others that one has genuine feelings towards?

Why Pride and Prejudice of course!

Pride and Prejudice

What a brilliant title that is for a book about the human condition! It still has the ability to shock and awe today despite its setting in the apparently genteel atmospheres of refined and cultured society and its attendant manners and courtesies. Who can forget the bouts of Mr Darcy fever when it was screened on television not so many years ago?

It is said that it was pride that caused Lucifer's fall from grace because he compared himself to God and wanted to be as powerful as God. As it says in the Bible:

"Your heart became proud on account of your beauty, and you corrupted your wisdom because of your splendour."

Lucifer became so impressed with his own beauty, intelligence, power, and position that he began to desire for himself the honour and glory that belonged to God alone. The sin that corrupted Lucifer was self-generated pride.

It is said that pride comes before a fall and Lucifer's story contains a clear moral that confirms the fact.

But alongside the saying of pride leading to a fall it could be said that pride leads to prejudice.

How can it lead to anything else?

For pride blurs the truth, the reality, the feelings, the emotions, the desires, the needs, the appetites and the humanities that make us human.

Pride is the harbinger of the ego and the ego sees only itself as the centre of its own and everything else's universe.

Pride is unbalanced, biased and warped, and anything with those eyes can only be prejudiced about what it sees

Prejudice means to pre-judge something before being fully aware of the facts about it. It relies on opinion, hearsay, innuendo, rumour, stereotyping and of course judgement. It is derived from the Latin "praeiudicium" which means judgement or previous damage.

To make decisions about things and other people based on judgement and / previous damage caused or inflicted is never a good idea because such places are unbalanced, unreliable, unstable and unsafe.

In short, prejudice isn't neutral or earthed in the sense that an electrical circuit needs a neutral or earth wire to make it safe to handle.

Why would it be any different for a human being?

Pride and prejudice make us unsafe to handle whereas tenderness of the heart makes us open and kind and safe to be with.

Alongside every human being there should a notice that often comes with a valuable item that is delivered to us.

And that note would say:

Handle with care.

Glass breaks extremely easily if not handled very carefully.

Who is to say that it is any different with a human heart?

'Tis the business of little minds to shrink; but he whose heart is firm, and whose conscience approves his conduct, will pursue his principles unto death.

Thomas Paine

Thomas Paine was not a bland man. Nor did he live what could be called in any way a bland, insipid, grey or boring life.

Born in Norfolk in in England in 1737, he was involved in some of the major revolutionary movements that occurred in the late 18th century, including both the French and American Revolutions. Not as an outsider looking in, but as insider looking both inwards and outwards from what he believed and perceived to be core fundamental truths about the human condition.

His life could easily be termed that of being a radical, but such an easy label does a tremendous disservice to a life that was committed, principled, bold, daring, and courageous and so much more.

The above quotation is not something uttered from the mouth of a pontificating intellectual, but is forged out from the coal face of his life's experience which was a truly remarkable life in very many ways.

He was a champion of causes, principles and values that he passionately believed in and espoused, wrote about and acted upon. In no way was he ever going to be a party political animal and nor would he allow his loyalties to be governed by either the land of his birth, nor tradition, custom and practice and assumed truths based on history, exploitation or vested interest.

To "the establishment" Thomas Paine was a very dangerous man indeed.

It is almost hard to believe from his portrait that this man from a very simple background in rural England was one of the most loved and loathed in equal measure men of the 18ᵗʰ century.

Yet one can see the long gaze of his eyes that they are both incredibly focused and penetrating at the same time. This is not a man who treats things lightly or superficially and nor is he himself someone to be treated lightly or trivially either for to do so would underestimate him and his abilities. As his life progressed his friends and enemies grew to know that they could not afford to do this because if they did it would be at the own peril, which often it was.

Although not nearly as well known today as many other key figures of what has come to be known as The Enlightenment, in his day Paine was as well-known and as influential as nearly anybody for his thought, philosophy, political theory and revolutionary ideas.

A dangerous man with dangerous ideas he was called by some.

His background contributed to his character formation, for he was born into a simple and hard-working Quaker family and as such was schooled strongly in core Quaker values of hard work, freedom of thought, freedom of religious worship and the fundamental rights of the individual. This was coupled with the need for a social contract requiring the individual to contribute to the greater good of society, and for society in return to fully reciprocate and recognise the rights of the individual.

He started life from humble beginnings as it seems he had very little formal education, and he began his working life very early helping his father make ropes or stays as they were called for shipping. But education was still a very important part of Quaker life and so it is highly probable he was given a good education at home in both reading and writing, but also in being schooled towards independent and critical thinking; a skill which he obviously developed to an exceptional degree. He no doubt used these skills to improve himself and his prospects and he seemed to achieve this at least initially.

Married at a young age, tragedy struck early for Paine for both his wife and child died when she was giving birth to their first child. Not only that, but his business failed soon afterwards as well.

Using his education and versatile skills he then became in turn a schoolteacher, an excise officer and then ended up getting a job in Lewes, Sussex a town noted for its pro-republican sentiment going back to the time of the

English Civil War. It is here that Paine also starts to get involved in civic affairs and political life.

However, his ability as a thinker and activist isn't apparently matched by his business skills as yet another business venture fails and he only narrowly avoids debtor's prison.

He then moves to London where he meets Benjamin Franklin who is much impressed by Paine and suggests that he should move to America. Franklin gives him a letter of recommendation that helps Paine travel there and introduces him to some contacts on his arrival in America in 1794.

He then becomes an editor and writer as well as being a designer, engineer and inventor and in 1796 he publishes his first major work titled *Common Sense*. This work has led many historians to label Paine as being the father of the American Revolution.

No lover of authority, monarchy, despots and vested interests, this work by Paine is an attack on the English Crown, its monarchy and its perceived unjust and parochial treatment of its colonists in America.

Paine wrote in a plain, non-literary, non erudite way that made his work and ideas expressed within it accessible to all colonists, even if they couldn't read or write, because it could be read in houses, meeting rooms and taverns. Once people had heard the work they understood it and were hardly likely to disagree with its contents due to the privations the colonists all felt at the hands of their English masters.

He was preaching to the converted, but in a way that made "common sense" of their plight, grievances and situation together with a rally to action to do something about it. This they did shortly after the pamphlet was published. It is estimated that the pamphlet sold 100,000 copies on publication (in a country of less than 2 million people at the time) and that probably 500,000 were sold during the course of the Revolution itself, which is an extraordinary number.

Somehow, by using the title "Common Sense" and writing in the style he did about the subject matter, Paine managed to connect and empathise with the plight of the ordinary person. This then motivated them to take action on matters they felt deeply passionate about in their hearts.

Paine more than anyone disseminated the idea that independence from England might not only be necessary but also possible. His work struck a very powerful chord and resonated with the aggrieved colonists and also gave them a consolidated thesis around which to rally rather than dispersing into multitudinous factions consumed as much with fighting each other as their colonial masters.

Paine more than anyone else gave Americans a sense of identity and patriotism, which as we can see today in the 21st century is still alive and as powerful as ever.

This enabled them to rise up against their perceived oppressor and also court popular support for their cause abroad in countries like France to where he later travelled.

In 1770 Paine published *The American Crisis*, another pamphlet which was written with the aim of inspiring the American people in their battles against the British army. Washington regarded it as being an essential piece of propaganda and inspiration. So much so that he insisted that extracts were often read to the troops to inspire them.

It's easy to see why it inspired them when the first lines read:

> *"These are the times that try men's souls: The summer soldier and the sunshine patriot will, in this crisis, shrink from the service of their country; but he that stands it now, deserves the love and thanks of man and woman. Tyranny, like Hell, is not easily conquered; yet we have this consolation with us, that the harder the conflict, the more glorious the triumph. What we obtain too cheap, we esteem too lightly: it is dearness only that gives everything its value. Heaven knows how to put a proper price upon its goods; and it would be strange indeed if so celestial an article as freedom should not be highly rated."*

Some critics seek to dismiss Paine as being no more than a polemicist and rhetorician, but that would be to doubt his passion, sincerity and genuineness and his dedication and commitment to the cause and causes he believed in.

Certainly it struck a chord with his readers.

He was sent as an emissary to France at this time and is credited with helping to obtain vital funds to help equip the army in the war against the British.

After Independence was achieved, feeling his work was done in America, or perhaps looking for more adventure, Paine found himself back in London by 1787 just as things were moving inexorably towards revolution in France with similar sentiments developing in other

European countries, including England, on the back of the American experience.

Paine actually visited France in 1790, the revolution having begun in 1789, and was more than an eyewitness to events that were occurring there. On his return to England he wrote and sought to publish his next work, *Rights of Man* in 1791. He then returned to Paris, apparently on the advice of William Blake, whilst leaving the manuscript with his publisher.

To say it caused a stir would be a massive understatement. He then followed that up with *Rights of Man, Part the Second, Combining Principle and Practice* in 1792 and the impact of this was sensational in the truest meaning of that word.

Championing populist causes it polarised the country and gave birth to the rise of many reform societies seeking to change society from its old dogmas and vested interests. So incendiary was this work that the government waged a vendetta against Paine in any way that it could, and even had him tried and convicted in absentia for seditious libel. This offence carried the death penalty for Paine if he ever returned to England, which he never did.

Not only that, but despite being a champion of the French Revolution he was imprisoned there too during the *"reign of terror"* and only very narrowly escaped the guillotine.

He later met Napoleon who claimed that he slept with a copy of Rights of Man under his pillow and that everyone should read it.

Whilst initially a great endorser of Napoleon, Paine later saw Napoleon's descent into dictatorship and turned against him calling him the *"greatest charlatan who ever lived."*

It seems that Thomas Paine didn't court popular opinion nor did he seek popularity in the courts of temporal power.

He was, in a word, consistent. And true to his word.

He remained in France until 1802 when at the invitation of the then President and personal friend Thomas Jefferson he returned to America.

This is despite the fact that whilst living in France, Paine had also turned his sights on no less an icon of the American Revolution than George Washington, (who Paine thought had conspired in his imprisonment in France) calling him amongst other things vain, ungrateful and an incompetent commander. He wrote of Washington:

"The world will be puzzled to decide whether you are an apostate or an impostor; whether you have abandoned good principles or whether you ever had any."

Come on Thomas tell us what you really think!

Yet despite this PR gaffe, he did return to America where he lived out the rest of his life. He died somewhat appropriately in the part of New York City we know today as Greenwich Village which is famous for its artists, bohemian lifestyles, freedom seekers and independent thinkers.

It was an actual village in Paine's time and it still retains some of that feel today.

Perhaps Thomas Paine was the first truly free and independent thinker to live there?

As an interesting curio it is interesting that Paine's name at birth was in fact spelt Pain. He added the letter e at the end later. Is it in any way possible that the expression *"It pains me to say this but ....."* comes in fact from Thomas Pain/e?

It may of course be simply a coincidence, but if it is it is a very interesting one.

Except perhaps for this thought, and that it is that it didn't seem to pain Thomas Paine to speak what was on his mind and in his heart.

He doesn't seem to have suffered from small mindedness and nor did he shrink or shirk from the truth as he saw it.

He most certainly let his conscience be his guide and he stayed true to his principles all the way through his life.

The world is most certainly a different and better place for a man like him having been in it.

The Heart is Forever Inexperienced.

Henry David Thoreau

It is not known whether there were any other Henry Thoreau's who lived at the same time as Henry David Thoreau that required Henry David Thoreau to use his middle name of David to distinguish him from any other Henry Thoreau. If there was another Henry Thoreau it is doubtful, very doubtful that they could be confused in any other way.

For it is very unlikely that Henry David Thoreau could be mistaken for any other person yet alone another Thoreau. He was in fact christened David Henry Thoreau and it was after college that he changed the ordering of his names to Henry David Thoreau, and perhaps this was him making a statement that he would not have his life ordered by the will of others even down to the ordering of his name?

The words unique, individual and original are often over used to describe people who may well be elements of those things, but with Thoreau it was quite possible that they didn't go far enough!

There isn't a box, a label a category that is big enough or wide enough or even appropriate to describe the short, meteoric life of Henry David Thoreau for even the concept of a box represents the antithesis of all that Thoreau's life stood for and represented.

He didn't so much think and live outside the box, he rather thought and lived outside without any kind of box whatsoever! And whilst he did see that there were boxes of conformity and conditioning that govern our lives and reality, he very much lived and exampled his life from being with and within nature which he loved most dearly. He saw nature as being the best teacher we have if we are to live our lives, truthfully, honourably, richly and rewardingly.

Thoreau is variously described as being a philosopher, author, poet, naturalist, abolitionist, transcendentalist, resister, environmentalist, ecologist, polemicist, rhetorician and lots of other labels that people use when they really don't know how to describe someone who defies description! He is also sometimes described as being an anarchist, but that is both a lazy and incorrect label. Thoreau was much better than that, for he was much more for things that worked rather than against things that didn't.

Born in 1817 in Massachusetts he packed an awful lot into his short life of 44 years before he died in 1862, probably as a result of complications resulting from a life long struggle with tuberculosis.

He was born into a modest New England family. They must however have been probably what we might call today middle class, because his family was able to send him to Harvard where he studied such subjects as mathematics, philosophy, rhetoric, classics and science. No doubt as a result of this he received an excellent education and platform for his own thinking and outlook.

However, whereas most if not all of his contemporaries saw their university education as preparing them for roles within society such as lawyers, educators, businessmen, bankers, doctors and even the church, Thoreau was much more interested in the university of life and how that might take him into the wild and untamed unknown, rather than the life of university and academic study. He felt that that might imprison and condemn him to a life of the tamed, sanitised and soulless known.

Thoreau was already aware of the rebel gene within him, as his maternal grandfather Asa Dunbar led the first ever student rebellion in the colonies at Harvard in 1776.

Upon completing his studies Thoreau became a teacher in his home town of Concord, but he resigned after a short time because he refused to administer corporal punishment in breach of the school's policy to do so if the children erred. This was a rare and very progressive stance for the time.

He then set up his own education faculty with his brother John which they called the Concord Academy. Within the educational programmes they developed classes and processes that many educators even today would regard as being radical and even revolutionary. This included such things as nature walks and visits to local shops and businesses to find out what the people who worked there did and how they did it.

The school had to close after Thoreau's brother died, but it was not long after this that Thoreau met Ralph Waldo Emerson who was impressed by the young man, and encouraged him to write and mentored him in many ways, albeit sometimes in a slightly patronising way.

Nevertheless, this helped forge and form many of Thoreau's views and thoughts as he endeavoured to make his experiences real and not intellectual.

To this end he built himself a cabin in the woods so that he could experience for himself life in the woods and the wilds.

This led to him writing one of his seminal works called Walden Woods. In this writing Thoreau espouses many of his views about nature and the human condition and how we need to learn from nature rather than try to control or conquer it.

His other great work (although he was an incredibly prolific writer) was Resistance to Civic Government (sometimes also known as Civil Disobedience), which is perhaps why he is often thought of as being an anarchist.

This book sets out many of his ideas about the relationship between the individual and the state and explores the importance of the conscience and morality, and the duty of the individual to be free from the control and tyranny of the state. Because without their individuals being truly free how can society and the state regard themselves as being truly free either?

In an attempt to practice what he preached, and at Emerson's behest, Thoreau built himself a simple hut in the woods and lived in it for two years to see what nature and the woods had to teach him.

This picture shows a replica of the hut the that Thoreau built and lived in with a statue of him in the foreground.

It appears that the experiment taught him a lot. At least until his experiment in cloistered living within nature was bizarrely interrupted by a visit from the tax inspector! The tax inspector informed Thoreau that he owed the government six years of poll taxes, which Thoreau refused to pay. So instead of living in self chosen exile Thoreau was put in a governemnt chosen one of prison for refusing to pay his taxes. He was released when someone (reputedly his aunt) paid these back taxes without and against Thoreau's consent.

Thoreau is one of those fascinating individuals who defies classification. He had great skills as a surveyor, educator, thinker, inventor, geopgrapher, nature chronocler, writer, environmentalist, provocatuer, advocate of the rights of man including seeking the abolition of slavery, emancipator humanitarian and moralist. Ghandi regarded him as being a prime influence in him developing his own philosophy and called Thoreau: *"One of the greatest and most moral men America has produced."*

Whilst Thoreau wasn't himself a populist many since have sought to popularise his work or perhaps use his works as authority or mandate for their own populist or unpopular agendas.

Thoreau himself saw the danger of adopting extreme and extremist agendas, and as he developed his own creed on successful living he saw that there needed to be a balance between different and sometimes competing needs in order for a progressive future to be found. He realised that the needs of society and the individual needed to be collaborative, much in the same way that he came to realise that the needs of civilization and nature also needed to be mutually accepted and respected. If these forces could live in balance and harmony then a practical and balanced solution could be found.

As he lived his life he sought this balance first of all in himself, and how he conducted his relationships with those he cared about from family and acquaintances to the world of nature which he truly loved, revered and marvelled at.

Whether he was conscious of it or not Thoreau was part of a time, an era, a movement, a response, an evolution, an awareness, a consciousness that somehow sought to balance out the harder edges of what came to be called The Enlightenment. Yet in many ways it itself became the very opposite of what it professed to be.

Or more accurately perhaps, with the rise and growth of the scientific method and the Indutrial Revolution humans became more and more skilled at looking into the nature of reality as a thing, and seeing what and how things worked in a much more forensic and less mysterious and superstitious way. This in part was a very good thing, because the scientific method reveals a very different truth than a non scientific one. But it doesn't necessarily reveal all of the truth, and indeed may suppress and evern deny some aspects of that truth.

In other words, we could look at the rise of The Enlightenment and the scientific method as being a shift in centre of gravity from the heart to the head, from the right side of the brain to the left and from the yin to the yang and the feminine to to the masculine.

As one of the great prioneers and advocates of the scientific method Isaac Netwon told us – for each and every action there is an equal and opposite reaction – and so around the rise to dominance of this scientific method, which still exists in our world today, there arose things like Romanticism, Transcendentalism, Existentialism, together with influencs from Eastern philosophy and religion emerging into, and merging with, Western culture.

Thoreau was a contemporary with some pretty amazing people including Ralph Waldo Emerson, Emily Dickenson, Walt Whitman, Henry Wadsworth Logfellow Edgar Allen Poe, William Wordsworth and following on from people like Byron, Shelley and his wife Mary who wrote Frankestein, and Keats and more including artists like Turner and Constable.

People who somehow kept alive the power and the message from the other side of ourselves. People who were often mostly regarded as being outsiders, but who were really urging and encouraging their fellow humans to find and listen to the insider of themselves. The other them that they were fearful of and had often locked up in prison and then thrown away the key.

Thoreau certainly found and touched this part of himself and the human experience and made his peace with this place he found.

When he was dying his Aunt Louisa asked him if he had made his peace with God, to wich Thoreau replied:

"I did not know we had ever quarreled."

Thoreau was a true visionary in many senses of that word for he could see the world both as it really was and also where it would go if we followed certain lines of possibility on the one hand where it might lead if we followed others.

His words and works are just as important and valid as they were when they were written.

And whilst sometimes quotations out of context do a disservice to the author, perhaps in this context some of those quotations from a wonderful human being might just do a service to you the reader in your search for your inner and outer truth?

But first here is a picture of Henry David Thoreau taken in 1856 to ponder over and contemplate.

Just who and what was this man? What moved him and why?

And can any of that move you too?

And now for some of those quotations:

"Most of the luxuries and many of the so-called comforts of life are not only not indispensable, but positive hindrances to the elevation of mankind."

"It's not what you look at that matters, it's what you see."

"Never look back unless you are planning to go that way."

"Most men lead lives of quiet desperation and go to the grave with the song still in them."

"What lies behind us and what lies ahead of us are tiny matters compared to what lives within us."

"We need the tonic of wildness...At the same time that we are earnest to explore and learn all things, we require that all things be mysterious and unexplorable, that land and sea be indefinitely wild, unsurveyed and unfathomed by us because unfathomable. We can never have enough of nature."

"As you simplify your life, the laws of the universe will be simpler; solitude will not be solitude, poverty will not be poverty, nor weakness."

"Heaven is under our feet as well as over our heads."

"What's the use of a fine house if you haven't got a tolerable planet to put it on?"

And lots, lots more.

Our 21st century hubris can cause us to look back with a jaundiced eye and think that perhaps Thoreau was very prescient and maybe ahead of his time.
But who knows, perhaps he was ahead of ours?

As for the quotation at the beginning of this chapter it is very enigmatic in many ways.

What does it mean that the heart is forever inexperienced?

Who really knows what Thoreau truly meant by this, but could part of its meaning lie in the fact that the true feelings of the heart are always present in the here and now?

The heart doesn't know or understand history, hatred, regret or blame. It carries no familiarity of any kind whatsoever whether that be the kind that breeds contempt or any other kind.

The heart has never experienced before what it is experiencing right now in the most sacred moment of all called now.

And in that moment of ultimate inexperience we can love and be loved and we can free and be free.

For:

"Not until we are lost do we begin to understand ourselves."

I was never really insane except upon occasions when my heart was touched. Let my heart be still a moment and this mystery explore.

Edgar Allen Poe

Edgar Allen Poe was a near contemporary of Thoreau and was born in the same state of Massachusetts. Perhaps it is a coincidence or maybe a fashion of the time that both men are remembered by both forenames as well as their surnames (although Poe's middle of Allan is really a second surname due to the fact that he was orphaned when very young and adopted by a couple named Allen).

Both men died relatively young in their forties, with Poe just making it to that age before he died in 1849.

They both also had great difficulty in finding a comfortable balance living in the state of the outer world as it manifested compared to the inner world that they touched by, were moved by and longed for.

Poe in particular had great difficulty in this struggle and his life was a continual flirtation between the light and dark of genius and madness, insight and despair, hope and hopelessness, sobriety and alcoholism, profundity and the profane, life and death.

Primarily remembered these days perhaps for his poem The Raven and his perceived predilection for the dark, saturnine, melancholic, macabre take on life, Poe was in fact a complex character and his writing is much more nuanced than that.

Possibly he is regarded in this way because he was a pioneer of what we consider today to be the short story and he really was one of the first if not the first to write in the genre we now call the detective story.

He had a very meticulous and detailed mind and was able to write in this way because he was very exacting in his approach to what he regarded as being the science of writing. He certainly didn't belong to the beige or grey group of writers or people, and was very black and white in his views across a spectrum of topics and genres.

Given the swings within both his nature and his writing it is possible today to consider that Poe may have been bi-polar or even manic depressive.

This would fit within the saturnine aspects of his personality which may not be surprising to some given that Poe was a Capricorn and that the ruling planet of Capricorn is Saturn which is in some aspects to do with old age and the fact of time itself. Saturn is associated with the god Cronos and we think of him today as being Old Father Time. For although he was only 40 when he died Poe seemed to carry the weight of the world on his shoulders at times and conveyed the impression of being a lot older than his carnal years.

Cronos is often depicted as carrying a scythe and this is interpreted as representing the Grim Reaper, the one who takes things away, be it that which doesn't fit within a life or the very fact of life itself.

Things can be absolute, final and very black and white for personalities who have such a strongly influencing saturnine aspect in their character which Poe most certainly did. He was prone to bouts of revelation and insight on the one hand and depression, alienation and escapism on the other.

The other aspect of the scythe it that it sweeps away in a very cutting way that which is regarded as being necessary to be cut down, harvested or simply removed. Again Poe had these aspects in full measure because he either agreed with something or someone but if he didn't then he was absolute in his dismissal of that which he regarded as being lesser, wrong or just plain rubbish.

He doesn't seem to have had a neutral button in his life, but he certainly had a self-destruct one which he seems to have been very adept at pushing from time to time and ever more frequently as his life progressed.

He was a troubled soul with a troubled mind and no sorrows to seek in his life with tragedy never that far away from haunting his endeavours to succeed in life. In some ways Poe's writing mirrored his own struggles in life with his style of writing most commonly being referred as Gothic. This again reflects the saturnine aspects of his character in writing about big, heavy, sometimes dark and macabre subjects and he was not renowned for his happy themes and endings.

As is often said a picture is worth a thousand words and below is one of the very rare pictures of Poe which conveys as much of these features more than words can ever do.

There is something ethereal and other worldly about him and his gaze into and beyond the photographer's lens with a firm, fixed, long view stare that gives the impression of Poe's mind being somewhere else.

It is a very penetrating gaze and one gets the impression that it would be very uncomfortable being fixed by Poe's gaze for more than a very short time.

Yet it was these eyes that sought deeper truths to the reality of human existence and drove him in an at times obsessive search for the meaning of life beyond the outer veneer of common place and ordinary existence.

Poe was a pioneer of mystery writing and if he had managed to get round to writing an autobiography then that would have been a bigger mystery than all his other writing put together.

Poe was a complete enigma in life and in art.

To pigeon-hole Poe would be to do him a great disservice for he defied classification, and indeed hated it and strove to write in a style and about subject matters that transcended realms of classification and comparison. In this he could be regarded as part of the transcendentalist and romantic movements of the time, but never as an insider looking in nor an outsider looking out, but perhaps an outsider looking out!

Another of Poe's lesser known works published shortly before his death is entitled Eureka. Poe regarded it as being a prose poem and it is his opus take on life, the universe and everything it.

It was panned in its day as being the ravings of a madman due to its elliptical and elusive style. Yet it is remarkably prescient in many ways and way ahead of its time in terms of perceptions about cosmology and even pre-dating later mainstream scientific theories on the origins of the universe such as the big bang theory.

The sub-title of Eureka is termed: *"An Essay on the Material and Spiritual Universe"* and Poe then sets out his premise and stall in the overview that follows.

Here are the first few lines that follow the headings:

> *"IT is with humility really unassumed it is with a sentiment even of awe that I pen the opening sentence of this work: for of all conceivable subjects I approach the reader with the most solemn the most comprehensive the most difficult the most august.*
>
> *What terms shall I find sufficiently simple in their sublimity sufficiently sublime in their simplicity for the mere enunciation of my theme?*

I design to speak of the Physical, Metaphysical and Mathematical of the Material and Spiritual Universe:—of its Essence, its Origin, its Creation, its Present Condition and its Destiny. I shall be so rash, moreover, as to challenge the conclusions, and thus, in effect, to question the sagacity, of many of the greatest and most justly reverenced of men.

In the beginning, let me as distinctly as possible announce not the theorem which I hope to demonstrate for, whatever the mathematicians may assert, there is, in this world at least, no such thing as demonstration but the ruling idea which, throughout this volume, I shall be continually endeavouring to suggest.

My general proposition, then, is this:—In the Original Unity of the First Thing lies the Secondary Cause of All Things, with the Germ of their Inevitable Annihilation.

In illustration of this idea, I propose to take such a survey of the Universe that the mind may be able really to receive and to perceive an individual impression."

This is not a treatise for the weak or faint hearted, and perhaps gives an excellent context for the two quotations from Poe at the start of the chapter to do with the heart.

For if one is to journey into these cosmological, universal and spiritual realms then one has to be prepared to dance with angels and blur the lines of reality and fantasy, sanity and insanity, reality and unreality, truth and fiction and the known and the unknown.

Poe is a more than willing journeyman into these realms and his quotations attest to that fact.

The first quotation states that Poe was never "really" insane except when his life was touched by something.

What does Poe mean by "insane" and what does he mean by "touched"?

Curiously enough the word touched as well as having its obvious literal meaning of being physically touched by someone or something also has connotations of being touched by either genius or madness or both. Poe would obviously rather be touched by something higher than ordinary life existence even if this means running the risk of going mad because the reward of possible revelation and enlightenment makes the risk a worthwhile one.

Here are some more quotes from Eureka which are amazing in that they predate our modern understandings of atomic and sub-atomic theory. Even after the atom was split the material universe was still thought to be made up of finite "particles" as opposed wave theory that postulates that everything is energy and that all energy appears to originate from a single point of origin.

Attraction and repulsion are the sole properties through which we perceive the universe.

Every atom attracts every other atom.

Does not so evident a brotherhood amongst atoms point to a common parentage?

Also that every atom resonates and "knows" every other atom.

The means of omnipotence and omniscience is exactly adapted to its purposes.

These are amazing insights that probably ensured that Poe was dismissed or ignored by the prevailing scientific wisdom of the time, and probably guaranteed that his work would be consigned to the quickly forgotten shelf.

Yet his awareness of the common origin of all things predates Darwin's theory of evolution through natural selection as does his awareness that everything vibrates and resonates and so affects and is affected by everything else. Today we call this the butterfly wing effect.

Given his notation that everything moves, this might explain why Poe longed for his beating heart to be still for just a moment so that he may explore the mystery of it all?

A moment's stillness inside the ebb and flow and flux of a universe teeming with life and intelligence might reveal more of truth and cause than all the libraries in the world a thousand times over ever could.

Poe touched the membrane and felt something from the other side of the membrane here on Earth.

He truly had his eureka moment.

Was it real?
Was it all a fantasy?
Was it truth?
Was it mad?
Was it God?
Was it nothing?

Was it in fact perhaps all of this and so much more?

Where the mind is biggest, the heart, the senses, magnanimity, charity, tolerance, kindliness, and the rest of them scarcely have room to breathe.

Virginia Woolf

Born in the latter part of the Victorian era in 1882 in Hyde Park Gate central London Virginia Woolf was part of what has now become famous as being the Bloomsbury Set in the small area around the British Museum in Holborn, London. Made up of influential writers, philosophers, artists and intellectuals, they were almost as famous for being famous as they were for any of their works. They were very influential in their day during the first half of the 20th century, and were probably London's equivalent at that time for what New York had in the 1950's and 60's and onwards to even today in Greenwich Village.

The main difference being that The Bloomsbury Set were predominantly from the English upper classes and not nearly as bohemian (although they probably liked to think that they were) as those who gravitated towards Greenwich Village who tended to be more poets, beatniks, oddballs and outsiders.

The Bloomsbury Set were insiders who were in the main extremely well educated, (most of the men in it were educated at Cambridge University) and were more determiners of style, fashion, trends of every kind from literature to economics to politics, and all round arbiters of taste in a very English way and very, very civilised about it too!

Members of the Bloomsbury Set included Virginia Woolf and her husband Leonard, who was an essayist and non-fiction writer, the economist John Maynard Keynes, the novelist E. M. Forster, the writer Lytton Strachey, Vanessa Bell the Post-Impressionist painter and her husband the art critic Clive Bell, Roger Fry a Post-Impressionist painter and art critic, Duncan Bell another Post-Impressionist painter and Desmond McCarthy a literary journalist.

These were in the main the core of this very influential group of writers, artists, thinkers and philosophers with a world famous economist thrown in for good measure. But the were many others in and around this group whose lives intersected with them in many ways and often met with them and these included people like T. S. Eliot, Vita Sackville West, Katharine Mansfield and others.

They were famous for pioneering new ways of thinking, writing and art, critical analysis and thought and rejecting the outdated mores and conformities of the Victorian era, and they believed powerfully in individual freedom and choice and rejected all forms of controls that sought to be imposed by social conventions.

However, it is very easy to see that they were very much insiders looking in rather than out because they didn't have any working class people within their set which was drawn from a very narrow niche of English upper class and professional society. They could afford to pontificate about such matters of artistic and literary merit because they were born into a world of social privilege that gave them the luxury to point out the failings of just such a world!

They wrote about, painted and gave opinions on what they knew about, and became not only famous for it but got very well paid for it too!

As E. M. Forster (who wrote A Passage to India) wryly observed about the Bloomsbury Set: *"In came the nice fat dividends, up rose the lofty thoughts."*

Without being too cynical about the possible hypocrisy within their approach, nevertheless they were highly influential in their day and they did genuinely want to change society for the better. They based this change upon rejection of bourgeois habits and values and wanted to rely instead on aesthetics, ethics, the intrinsic value and worth of things rather than moralities and guilt that may surround them, and the importance of love and personal relationships as the criteria for the merit of one's actions.

Lofty aspirations indeed, and in many ways self-authorising and self-indulgent and more than a little naïve and insular.

As Keynes himself reflected some years later after repudiating many of his earlier held views when he was part of the group: *"We completely misunderstood human nature, including our own."*

Yet they had some very radical and liberal thinkers and some very brilliant minds, which is rather appropriate given the quote from Virginia Woolf that introduces this chapter. Because sometimes a brilliant mind is just as likely to get a person into trouble and difficulty as it is to getting them out of it.

No doubt Virginia's upbringing contributed much to her thought processes, philosophy, writing genre and style. For she herself came from a very bohemian, unusual and highly unorthodox background.

Virginia was born Adeline Virginia Stephen to Sir Leslie Stephen and his wife Julia Prinsep Duckworth Stephen, both of whom had been married and widowed before they married each other. There was an age difference of about 14 years between them and both brought children from these previous marriages before they went on to have four more children together, including Virginia.

Therefore, there were children from three sets of marriages all living in the same house at various times, which makes for a very complex set of family dynamics and relationships. It seems to have had a very profound and troubling effect on Virginia.

Her half-sister Laura from her father's previous marriage suffered from mental instability from before the time Virginia was born, but lived with the family until 1891 when she officially declared mentally disabled and institutionalised. It seems that Virginia inherited some of the highly strung, fragile and volatile nature of her half-sister, and no doubt as a young girl she was also highly influenced by her sister's inability to cope in the outer world. This struggle would continually play itself out throughout Virginia's own life.

Her father was a renowned, author, historian and critic and he founded The Dictionary of National Biography. Her mother could be seen to be a forerunner of all the Bloomsbury Set aspired to be. She was born in India during the time of The Raj, later returned to England to further her education, and became acquainted with the group known as The Pre-Raphaelite Brotherhood (a group of eminent artists) and was the model used within some of their works, notably those of Edward Burne-Jones.

With such well-connected parents the Spencer household was a mecca for famous people coming and going, and a rich and diverse upbringing it most certainly was. But it was hardly a very structured, normal or stable one, especially as Virginia was educated at home. For whilst it was no doubt excellent in many ways, it wasn't normal because Virginia didn't really meet with and mix with any children of her own age and get to learn through shared learning and play. Rather, she learned from adults about the adult world and whilst she marvelled at it, she never really grew properly into it.

It seems that Virginia longed to be loved as much as she loved.

Virginia suffered the first of her numerous mental breakdowns or "episodes" around the time that her mother died in 1895 when she was 13. She recovered somewhat and was able to continue her education at King's College London where she met some eminent reformers of women's education who were possibly the precursors of the Suffragette Movement that followed a decade later.

When her father died in 1904 she suffered an even worse mental disintegration and had to be institutionalised for a time. It is said that a large contribution to her state was the fact that she and her sister were sexually abused by their older half-brothers. If true, this obviously added to her already very frail state of mind, and coupled with the death of her parents and sister probably tipped Virginia over the edge.

She did make a partial recovery and her love of art and literature helped her in this. This enabled her to move in well-educated and highly connected circles. She married Leonard in 1907 and they lived in Gordon Square, Bloomsbury. It seems that the marriage was a close one and largely successful, and they remained together until Virginia's death by suicide in 1941. Leonard appears to have offered Virginia lots of support during the turbulent periods of her life which were frequent. This is despite the fact that Virginia had what appears to be an ongoing affair with Vita Sackville-West.

In modern terms it is quite possible that a clinical diagnosis of Virginia would assess her as being bi-polar or even manic depressive. She seems to have had periods of euphoria and creative generation coupled with other times of crippling self-doubt and depression. There doesn't seem to have been much of a half-way house between the two states of mind for her.

She wrote in different genres and styles and her works included novels, non-fiction and critical essays. Her work has been credited with being highly innovative in its style and subject matter and she is regarded as being one of the pioneers of what is termed stream of consciousness alongside James Joyce and E. M, Forster.

Given the mental issues that she suffered from for most of her life it seems that this ability to traverse the worlds between the conscious and the unconscious, the real and the fiction, the constructed and deconstructed was both a blessing and a curse. For it not only gave her access to a great freedom with her experimental style and themes, it also created a prison in her own mind from which she couldn't escape. Ultimately the prison became unbearable and tragically she decided to take her own life.

Her final note to Leonard makes for a particularly sad, poignant, moving goodbye.

Dearest, I feel certain that I am going mad again. I feel we can't go through another of those terrible times. And I shan't recover this time. I begin to hear voices, and I can't concentrate. So I am doing what seems the best thing to do. You have given me the greatest possible happiness. You have been in every way all that anyone could be. I don't think two people could have been happier till this terrible disease came. I can't fight any longer. I know that I am spoiling your life, that without me you could work. And you will I know. You see I can't even write this properly. I can't read. What I want to say is I owe all the happiness of my life to you. You have been entirely patient with me and incredibly good. I want to say that—everybody knows it. If anybody could have saved me it would have been you. Everything has gone from me but the certainty of your goodness. I can't go on spoiling your life any longer. I don't think two people could have been happier than we have been. V

This background and context from Virginia's life and sad end gives location and access to some of the emotional longing that resonates with and from the quotation at the start of the chapter.

Virginia knew what it was like to mix with people who had brilliant minds. She spent all her life moving in such circles and whilst at times this could be incredibly powerful and literally heady, there comes a point when heady simply isn't enough. Mixing so much with the world of ideas, intellectual pursuits, words and brilliance doesn't generate of itself the simple qualities that a life needs to make it feel, loved, cared about and valued.

The quotation itself doesn't come from the mind of Virginia Woolf but from the very heart of her. Perhaps it was a cry from the essence of her being that needed the love and protection that could keep her safe from the assault of the world that seemed to lay siege upon her sanity?

Nobody has ever been able to isolate the mind or even find it in terms of it being a physical reality in the way that it is easy to find your big toe. The mind, like the soul, is a very elusive thing and very ephemeral. Yet everyone acknowledges that they have a mind and that it is very powerful in influencing all aspects of our existence.

It is even regarded as possibly being more powerful than physical things for we have expressions like: it is a case of mind over matter, make up your mind, it's all in the mind, the power of the mind and many more.

Although the mind can be powerful and influential, it can also at times be an interference, and instead of providing insight and revelation it causes noise and blockage and thereby prevents the flow of a natural, genuine and human response.

A baby doesn't need its mother to read to it from a book about infant care. It needs its mother to cuddle it, suckle it, love and cherish it, bond with it and to keep it safe and warm. Reading the baby a copy of War and Peace, or discussing the relative merits of Impressionist and Renaissance art aren't going to help address the primary needs of the baby. A nappy being changed will probably bring more pleasure than a lecture on the differences between existential and humanist philosophies.

Our minds are full of all sorts of incredibly useful and useless bits of information. It's useful to know how to tie a tourniquet round a heavily bleeding limb to prevent blood loss and possible death. It's not really that useful to know that the battle of Hastings was 1066.

The mind is not the lungs of our inner life. Nobody ever fell in love because of a bunch of statistics. It is doubtful that the Good Samaritan helped every 9th person that he came across who needed assistance. The Buddha didn't develop compassion because it seemed like a good idea or because it was good career move.

The qualities that Virginia Woolf speaks of are ethereal but real, intangible but tangible, near but far and as vital and vitalising as the very air that we breathe. But like ourselves they too need room to breathe. For when we live in cramped, overcrowded and polluted environments we suffer and become ill.

Who is to say that it is any different for the inner worlds of the spirit and soul and the truth of who and what we really are?

Virginia Woolf touched those worlds and felt the agony and the ecstasy of to have and to have not these things close by and far away.

It is better to have felt what it is like to have and not have these things in your life rather than never having felt them at all.

Isn't a moment of having experienced magnanimity, charity, tolerance and kindness far better than all the words sitting in books in the British Library?

Maybe it's time to listen to Virginia Woolf's cry and plea and realise that whilst all the best minds can help change the world for the better, it is our hearts that will allow the world to change ourselves for the better.

The human heart has hidden treasures. In secret kept, in silence sealed. The thoughts, the hopes, the dreams, the pleasures, whose charms were broken if revealed.

Charlotte Bronte

Charlotte Bronte was a 19th century English novelist who was born and grew up in the county of Yorkshire. Although with Yorkshire being the way it is with it being probably the most parochial of all the English counties perhaps many there regard her as being a good Yorkshire lass who also happened to be English!

She was of a similar age to Queen Victoria and so was a contemporary of the queen. However, whilst Victoria lived to the ripe old age of 81 and ruled for over 63 years, Charlotte died at the relatively young age of 38 in 1855. This was at the height of Victoria and Albert's influence into English society and with the British Empire being at the peak of its power.

It is in this context that Charlotte lived before Victoria lost Albert, a few years after Charlotte's own death, and Victoria's retreat into mourning as the *"Widow of Winsor"*. This led to, at least in part, to what we now term Victorian moralities and sensibilities, which could perhaps be characterised with the saying: *"We are not amused."*

However, before that time England enjoyed a time of prolific expansion and growth in all realms of its Empire, for it is in this time that Britain starts to consider itself

"Great" Britain and Victoria is declared to be Empress of India. All manners of growth occurred and it was era of great discoveries in science, the arts flourished, commerce boomed and optimism abounded and the world was a plentiful and abundant place. Britain led the way in these pioneering times with people like Isambard Kingdom Brunel, Michael Faraday and others being the flag bearers of a brave new era.

Or so it seemed. For alongside the Industrial Revolution and all its new science, new methods and new possibilities, there was also a deep social division within society. For whilst some found great wealth and riches, there also developed great inequality, poverty, hunger (the Great Famine in Ireland, which was still part of Great Britain in those days, happened early in Victoria's reign), social injustice (women could not vote and very few of the male population could either). Plus, with more and more people moving to live in cities and away from the land, England began shifting from being a "green and pleasant land" to one that was dominated by industrial and heavily polluted landscapes and often squalid cities.

This social unrest was epitomised by the fact that there were a number of assassination attempts made on Victoria's life early in her reign by people who were disaffected, not so much by Victoria herself personally, but by what she represented in term of the privilege and class system and all it stood for.

It shouldn't be forgotten that around the time of Victoria and Charlotte's birth there was what has come to be termed The Luddite Rebellion and this a was a powerful protest movement by many artisans and tradesmen against the increased mechanization and industrialization of work practices. Whilst this was increasing production in an exponential way, it was at the expense of thousands of jobs and was thus undermining the livelihoods of many skilled workers.

This movement was very much against the process of mechanization, and saw this process as a threat to livelihoods and the communities that the artisans and tradesmen lived in. It had much popular support at the time. At one stage the government had more troops fighting the Luddites than it did have fighting wars on the continent of which there were many.

The Luddite rebellion was forcibly and brutally put down and suppressed. It is interesting however that we still have the term Luddite today and it carries a stigma in that anyone who is a Luddite is perceived as being anti-progress, anti-science, anti-technology, anti the future. A Luddite is a stick in the mud who should be mocked and ridiculed at worst, and looked as merely an anachronism and out of touch at best.

In many ways the time that Charlotte lived in was best encapsulated by Charles Dickens's opening lines from the novel a Tale of Two Cities:

> *"It was the best of times, it was the worst of times, it was the age of wisdom, it was the age of foolishness, it was the epoch of belief, it was the epoch of incredulity, it was the season of Light, it was the season of Darkness, it was the spring of hope, it was the winter of despair, we had everything before us, we had nothing before us, we were all going direct to Heaven, we were all going direct the other way - in short, the period was so far like the present period, that some of its noisiest authorities insisted on its being received, for good or for evil, in the superlative degree of comparison only.*

This was the world that Charlotte was born into, and lived her life in the early and middle 19ᵗʰ century.

She was born into a middle class family and was the third of six children, most of whom had health issues. Two of her sisters died in childhood of tuberculosis. Her sister Emily was the author of the even more famous novel Wuthering Heights and she herself died at the age of only 30 in 1848.

Charlotte suffered from delicate and fragile health all her life before her own death whilst she was pregnant. Yet despite dying at the age of only 38 in 1855 she in fact lived the longest of any of the six children.

She was very close to her siblings as they grew up. Together they created imaginary worlds and used their creative gifts to great effect in building these other worlds and societies and different relationships between the characters.

Charlotte then channelled this energy into writing a first novel that was called The Professor. She used the pen name Currer Bell as it wasn't really seen that writing novels was something that a young woman from polite society should be doing. This novel did not secure her a publisher, but undeterred she pressed on with her second novel which was called Jane Eyre, and the rest as they say is history.

Originally titled *"Jane Eyre – An Autobiography."* it is no exaggeration to state that the book revolutionised the genre of fiction in many ways. For it is written in a way that the central character is effectively narrating the novel from their viewpoint and perspective, and not only that but from a woman's point of view as well.

It is radical both in its style and subject matter, and it could in many ways be regarded as the first feminist novel. For it doesn't portray its central character as being a weak and docile member of the fairer and weaker sex in a one dimensional and dismissive way that most male writers had done previously. Jane is a complex, powerful and passionate woman with strong values, ideals and principles and is not someone to be trifled with.

For example, in the novel Jane only agrees to marry Mr Rochester on the basis that he agrees that the marriage will be between equals, and that she is to be regarded as no lesser than him in any way. This is way ahead of its time, for at that stage in Victorian England married women were not entitled to own any property and any property they did own became that of the husband automatically on their marriage. To all intents and purposes, the woman herself was regarded as effectively being the property of the man, and he could if he felt the need beat her and not be in breach of the law.

Jane is certainly not a member of the weaker sex and is strong willed, brave, courageous and determined, and when we read the book we are not accompanying Jane on the journey of becoming a doting and obedient domestic goddess of the 19th century.

Instead, we travel with Jane on her life's journey, and watch and witness as she develops her moral and spiritual code through the many experiences she has during the course of the book.

It is brilliantly written in that the style is easily accessible even today, and yet it explores complex and real issues and themes that we can identify with today, such as Jane's struggle with the relationship between doing one's duty, whether real or perceived, and the need for the pursuit of individual happiness. What is the right thing to do?

The book explores issues of social mores and moralities, class, love, power, control, gender relationships, stereotyping, roles, atonement, forgiveness and more in a way that was far ahead of its time. Yet in many ways it was also of its time and very much on time for it received popular reviews and sold well. Eventually Charlotte went public and admitted that she was in fact the author of the book.

It is quite probable that Jane is based on Charlotte herself, or at least Charlotte as she perceived herself or aspired to be. This is because Jane is independent, strong minded, determined, moral, is a champion of freedom and righteousness and has strong Christian values. Certainly these are attributes that Charlotte herself cherished and probably possessed herself.

It is sometimes said that if a person wishes to be successful in writing then they should stick to writing about what they now about. If so, it appears that Charlotte knew a great deal about the human condition for she writes about it in a wide, diverse, insightful, penetrating passionate and compassionate way with strength, conviction, intimacy, humanity and a gritty realism that was different from much of the escapist fantasy that was popular at the time. Chick Lit wasn't for Charlotte.

Curiously enough, Charlotte later faced some of the same issues in the book in her own life when she was trying to decide whether she should and if so who she might marry at the relatively late age of her mid-thirties.

Should she follow her heart or should she follow her head?

It seems that she found the same equilibrium that Jane was searching for when she married Arthur Bell Nicholls. Sadly, however, within a year of their marriage and whilst pregnant Charlotte became gravely ill and died, possibly of typhus.

In many ways Charlotte wrestled in Jane Eyre with what we might call today a classic battle between the head and the heart. Should one do what one's head tells one to do as being the "right" thing to do or should one follow one's heart and do things for love, passion and freedom?

It is clear that there is a balance to be found between the two, but that the leader of the balance needs to be the heart for that is where the greater power and the greater wisdom lies.

Charlotte has been called "the first historian of private consciousness" in the method and style that she used in Jane Eyre. In some respects, she is the forerunner of James Joyce, Marcel Proust and others in what later came to be termed the stream of consciousness style of writing.

Where the line of truth and fiction lies between Charlotte writing about a fictional character called Jane and her own private thoughts and consciousness is not clear, and this is what makes the appeal of her writing even greater. The marriage of the internal struggle between truth and duty and the universal themes of morality, principles, ethics, freedom and more reveal that Charlotte knew and wrestled with these themes in her own life. This is why she was able to write about them in such a captivating and revealing and true to life way.

With this quotation about the heart, Charlotte is saying that the heart isn't simply an organ that beats and pumps blood around the body. It is a home, a sanctuary, a place of most special feelings, emotions, hopes and desires. It is not a place to treat with anything other than reverence and respect, for it is where the truth of a person's feelings reside. It is sacred and spiritual in ways that the ordinary, everyday world does not understand and possibly doesn't believe, and therefore can easily be dismissed as being fantasy or trivial. But it is the place where the true connection to who and what we really are as human beings lies.

What does Charlotte mean when she says that the thoughts, the hopes, the dreams and the pleasures of the heart are broken if revealed?

Firstly, it is completely physically unprovable that the human heart can be a sanctuary or refuge for such things. Yet we do feel these things, and they have to live somewhere so why not the heart? New studies suggest that the heart indeed does at least respond to moments of intense emotion, and may be a storehouse or memory vault for these feelings and a link to them. In short the heart seems to indeed have a memory and trigger response mechanism.

Yet those are possible mechanistic explanations, and Charlotte clearly isn't speaking in such terms when she writes. She is speaking from the being side of being human, not the doing side. This is the sacred, spiritual, loving side of ourselves that makes us truly human. What we care about, cherish and hold dear about what we love and who we love that is beyond explanation, sometimes even unto ourselves.

This is the mystery and mystical side of ourselves, the transcendent, the romantic (in the truest and highest meaning of that word, and not the common meaning it mostly has today) and the essence of what makes the human experience divine and part of the divine.

This is the part that cannot be reduced to a chemical equation, nor explained in strictly rational terms. For to seek to do so lessens the experience and what causes the experience in the first place. God can't be put into a test-tube and nor can love.

We can no more calculate that we will fall in love than we can tickle ourselves! For when we try to tickle ourselves somehow the tickle response that we all have when someone else tickles us switches itself off.

Thoughts, hopes, dreams and pleasures exist in another dimension to the strictly carnal world of bones, bloods and nerves.

To reveal what these things are and how they work and where they come from and why, somehow breaks their magic and the spell they have over both ourselves and those we have these feelings about. No wonder the Magic Circle has an unwritten code that magician should never reveal to their audience how a trick is done because that ruins the magic. The art lies in the audience not knowing how the trick has been done, and them gasping in wonder at what seems to be impossible to the rational mind.

This is something that the German sociologist, philosopher and economist Max Weber was referring to when he spoke of escaping the iron cage of rationality. The ability to reason and use logic and rational thinking are great gifts, but also at times a prison from which we need to escape and find the true freedom that things like intuition, feeling, emotion, passion and love give us.

These are the secret, hidden treasures of the heart that are worth far more than all the gold in all the bank vaults in the world or more than all the tea in China! A cup of tea can be most refreshing indeed, but the secret, hidden treasures of the heart connect to the very elixir of life itself.

The unexplained and unexplainable are the only things that can explain everything about what makes the human experience truly human.

And for that we have a lot to thank Charlotte Bronte for.

When we die we live on in the hearts of others.

Carl Sagan

I first became aware of Carl Sagan in the early 1980's when he released the TV series entitled: *Cosmos: A Personal Voyage.*

This was an amazing, ground breaking series, for it used imagery and graphics that had never been seen before to give the viewer a much more tangible and visceral impression of what it feels like to be part of this great cosmos in which we find ourselves to be alive.

With Sagan's easy going and very accessible style of passing across profound science with an awe and wonder about the very fact of life itself, it is no wonder that the series became the most viewed ever in the history of public broadcasting with an estimated audience of over 500 million worldwide. I was more than delighted to be happily lost within a club of 500 million people whilst watching the series.

Today the graphics used would be considered to be somewhat primitive, crude and clunky, but at the time they were jaw-droppingly amazing and simply took one's breath away. It is easy to see looking back just how much of a pioneer Sagan was in being a pioneer communicator about the importance and beauty of science in explaining and understanding our world and universe. As such he was a trailblazer for later presenters such as Brian Cox with his various series on the BBC.

And whilst Cox has the advantage of the incredible progress that computers and digital technology have brought to the genre, there was something about Sagan himself that brought something essential to the process that added to the mystery and enigma of the very fact of life and how we got to be here.

With many of the modern science programmes there comes something of an agenda that somehow the mystery simply lies in the fact that science itself hasn't got the answer yet, but that ultimately science can and will be able to explain why things are the way they are. The beauty for them lies in the fact that science can explain all things because nature works by a series of laws. If one gets to understand what those laws like Gravity, Relativity, Quantum Theory, Big Bang, Inflationary Theory, the Standard Model, the Theory of Everything etc. then we can know all there is to know about our reality.

But there was something about how Sagan presented his series that left one not quite knowing where he stood about certain matters to do with philosophy and possibly religion, as opposed to him simply being a bottom line science geek who thought everything could be explained by physics, chemistry and biology.

For was Sagan an atheist, a theist or perhaps an agnostic? One was never quite sure where he stood on matters of faith and belief and whether or not he thought there was a purpose behind and to it all. Are we here because of mere happenstance or is there some kind of divine order and purpose to it all?

With other science presenters one often gets the not too hidden agenda that science is enough to fill all our needs regarding the explanations, reasons and purposes why we are here. With Sagan one was always left with questions that often got bigger as Carl walked us through the cosmos and introduced us all to our greater home.

He sternly resisted defining other people's reality, beliefs and faiths, and also resisted himself being classified as this or that label and would often answer questions about his own beliefs in seemingly contradictory ways.

Whatever his own personal creed and beliefs he was certainly brilliant at being a populariser of science, the awe of being alive and the passion and zest for finding out about why things are the way that they are and how we can live more rewarding, fulfilling and satisfying lives.

Whether you were a hard line atheist or a hard line deist he reeled you in and proved to one and all that the Universe and everything in it (including us) was amazing.

He also was passionately interested in finding out whether we are "alone" in the Universe and spent much of his time engaged in the search for extra-terrestrial life. He believed that the odds that we were alone as being the only planet with organic life on it in such a vast and teeming Universe were far greater than us not being alone. To this end in trying to contact other life forms, he was instrumental in assembling messages on the Pioneer and Voyager space programmes in case they were discovered by other life forms out there in space somewhere.

Sagan also wrote the novel Contact that was subsequently made into a film starring Jodie Foster.

In the film in the opening sequence it shows a young girl with a passionate interest in the stars and the Universe and wondering and hoping whether someone or something *"out there"* might respond to her ongoing attempts to make contact.

She asks her father in this opening scene:

"Dad do you think that people live on other planets?"

Her father looks kindly upon her in her desperate need to know and replies:

"I don't know Sparks, but if we are alone then that's an awful waste of space!"

It seems that Carl Sagan loved the fact that there were things he could know through the employment of sound scientific principles and rigour. He was passionate about applying these methodologies, not only to know what could be known, but also from a sound philosophical and moral standpoint to try and make this small blue planet we call home a better place for all.

He also loved the things that he didn't know, and rather than being dogmatic about these things or try and fill them with the wrong kinds of certainties he was comfortable with occupying a space between competing certainties and leave the matter to be resolved when the unknown becomes more known.

In this regard he didn't see that things such as science and religion needed to be mutually exclusive. He preferred a much more nuanced approach where the best of both could offer something to the other and thereby perhaps offer each other an opportunity for balance, humanity, perception, humility and truth.

Sagan clearly didn't believe in the idea of God being made in the image of ourselves for he said things like:

"The idea that God is an oversized white male with a flowing beard who sits in the sky and tallies the fall of every sparrow is ludicrous. But if by God one means the set of physical laws that govern the universe, then clearly there is such a God. This God is emotionally unsatisfying ... it does not make much sense to pray to the law of gravity."

Although if one falls out of a plane without a parachute it might pay to pray to the law of gravity for some relief, but to honest it is doubtful that those prayers would be answered!

Sagan wasn't impressed with the idea that there might be a God that was probably some kind of super-human looking and acting human somewhere in the sky, because to him that is all our human centric minds could stretch to in terms of their being some kind of order, reason and purpose to living.

However, it appears that he didn't hold much truck with what we might today call militant atheism either for he also said:

"An atheist is someone who is certain that God does not exist, someone who has compelling evidence against the existence of God. I know of no such compelling evidence. Because God can be relegated to remote times and places and to ultimate causes, we would have to know a great deal more about the universe than we do now to be sure that no such God exists. To be certain of the existence of God and to be certain of the nonexistence of God seem to me to be the confident extremes in a subject so riddled with doubt and uncertainty as to inspire very little confidence indeed."

Sagan was happy to leave the matter open because as both a scientist and humanist he could see that dogmatism and fundamentalism only lead to intellectual, philosophical, social, economic, political and religious conflict. And with all that noise coming from this planet in an escalating manner as we become more and more "*civilised*", what intelligent life form from elsewhere in the cosmos would try and get in contact with us if our only intention is to try and conquer it and / or destroy it if we don't destroy ourselves first?

He felt that all such views could be accepting and acceptable to each other provided they help improve the human condition. For example, this is what he had to say about the relationship between science and spirituality:

"Science is not only compatible with spirituality; it is a profound source of spirituality. When we recognize our place in an immensity of light-years and in the passage of ages, when we grasp the intricacy, beauty, and subtlety of life, then that soaring feeling, that sense of elation and humility combined, is surely spiritual."

We are not just the sum of our parts, even if the sum of our parts are as vast as the very cosmos itself.

We cannot understand who and what we are and why we are here simply by understanding the stuff of which we are made.

We are made of genes but it wasn't genes that made us and nor do they define who and what we are and what we can be and do in our entirety.

Sagan advocated that we use scientific and critical thinking in our search for truth but he also recognised that there were other parts of ourselves that mathematical or chemical equations alone could not explain or dismiss.

What mattered most was that we used all tools and methods available to us to help us make informed and responsible decisions about our reality both for ourselves and the future of our planet and our species and all the other species we share the Earth with.

In this regard one of the seminal and most popular writings of Sagan (since called *"The Pale Blue Dot"*) was inspired by a photograph taken in 1990 by the Voyager 1 probe of Earth from a record-breaking distance of 6.1 billion kilometres.

In it, the Earth only appeared as a single pale blue pixel. This inspiring and humbling picture has been described as one of the most important astronomical pictures ever taken. Even though it showed no new science it did something much more important, it reminded us all how precious and small Earth really is. Here is what Carl Sagan had to say about it.

"Look again at that dot. That's here. That's home.
That's us. On it everyone you love, everyone you
know, everyone you ever heard of, every human
being who ever was, lived out their lives. The
aggregate of our joy and suffering, thousands of
confident religions, ideologies, and economic
doctrines, every hunter and forager, every hero and
coward, every creator and destroyer of civilization,
every king and peasant, every young couple in love,
every mother and father, hopeful child, inventor and
explorer, every teacher of morals, every corrupt
politician, every "superstar," every "supreme leader,"
every saint and sinner in the history of our species
lived there-on a mote of dust suspended in a
sunbeam.

The Earth is a very small stage in a vast cosmic
arena. Think of the endless cruelties visited by the
inhabitants of one corner of this pixel on the scarcely
distinguishable inhabitants of some other corner, how
frequent their misunderstandings, how eager they are

to kill one another, how fervent their hatreds. Think of the rivers of blood spilled by all those generals and emperors so that, in glory and triumph, they could become the momentary masters of a fraction of a dot.

Our posturings, our imagined self-importance, the delusion that we have some privileged position in the Universe, are challenged by this point of pale light. Our planet is a lonely speck in the great enveloping cosmic dark. In our obscurity, in all this vastness, there is no hint that help will come from elsewhere to save us from ourselves.

The Earth is the only world known so far to harbour life. There is nowhere else, at least in the near future, to which our species could migrate. Visit, yes. Settle, not yet. Like it or not, for the moment the Earth is where we make our stand.

It has been said that astronomy is a humbling and character-building experience. There is perhaps no better demonstration of the folly of human conceits than this distant image of our tiny world. To me, it underscores our responsibility to deal more kindly with one another, and to preserve and cherish the pale blue dot, the only home we've ever known."

One might agree or disagree with some or all of what Sagan has to say or perhaps suggest that his view is a tad negative towards the tally of our contribution to the history of life on this planet. But then again we do have "form" so he has a point.

Whatever one's view of Sagan what is hard to disagree with is the way that he puts the reality of our experience into a far greater context than might normally be the case.

Our inflated sense of self-importance is even smaller than the tiny dot in the picture we all share as home.

So before we go off and conquer the rest of the Universe, have we really yet come to appreciate the true beauty, awesome balances and sacredness of life as exists here on Earth?

As an Irish farmer said to me many years ago when I was seeking directions to the next destination on my journey:

"What's wrong with here?"

Perhaps NASA one day might launch a mission to Earth and conduct some experiments to see if the Earth is a suitable place for human beings to colonise and occupy in the future? Think of all the money they would save on fuel!

Voyager gave us another set of eyes to see what life looks like from far away. Maybe there are another set of eyes that we can use to see what our reality is like from up close and personal if we can somehow see both the wood and the trees at the same time?

It seems that Sagan was comfortable with the view that science, art, philosophy and religion could all offer each other complementary views into and out from the nature of reality in our search for truth.

Otherwise he wouldn't say:

"When we die we live on in the hearts of others."

Science tells us that energy cannot be created or destroyed, it can only change its form.

Our hearts also know this to be true because those people and things we care about deeply and love without requirement and condition resonate within us, and we become a home for them whist we are alive.

Where do these feelings come from and originate from? Other people? The Planet? The very cosmos itself?

The heart of the matter can sometimes only be seen from afar and The Pale Blue Dot is a proof that this is true.

Yet other times the truth of the matter can only be seen from the heart.

No wonder the ancients said that if you want to understand the human study the Universe and if you want to understand the Universe study the human.

This is a view that I am sure Carl Sagan would have endorsed.

His life certainly wasn't a waste of space, in the spirit of the line from the film, because with all his life experiences, his hopes, fears, successes and mistakes he added to the richness of our human experience and made the lives of millions better for having been here.

His life, and indeed everyone else's life of all who have ever lived, might in fact add up to and mean nothing when the final tally is made.

But then again it might.

One thing is sure though, and that it most certainly won't matter or make any difference if that life isn't in fact lived in the first place. For nothing can live on in the hearts of others if nothing lives in the heart of the person they love.

Nature abhors a vacuum and so does love.

Better therefore to have love in your life and for life rather than a vacuum unless of course the house needs cleaning! ☺

I prosper that it is better to have a heart without words than words without a heart.

John Bunyan

John Bunyan was a 17th century English writer and preacher who is probably best remembered for his book The Pilgrim's Progress. However, he was far from being a one trick pony. For whilst he may be remembered for the power and the moral and religious themes contained within the book, it is clear from his life story that he lived in profound times and contributed more than his fair share of energy, passion and commitment towards being an agency for change.

The moral, spiritual and philosophical truths that he believed in and was prepared to pay the necessary price of to see those beliefs championed were enshrined not just in his book, but also in his life.

Born near Bedford in 1628, it seems that he had little formal schooling but that he attended the University of Life instead. He lived in truly revolutionary times in every sense of the word for this was when the king of England, King Charles I and parliament were engaged in a fierce struggle for power. This eventually led to the English Civil War which in turn resulted in the overthrow of the King and his execution.

Bunyan must have been aware of this struggle from his earliest years, and indeed he joined the Parliamentary army in 1644 when he was a mere 16 years of age. This was in the earlier stages of the conflict and he spent the next three years fighting the parliamentary cause before returning home in about 1647.

There is no definitive proof as to what Bunyan did during his period of active service it is hard to believe that it didn't have a profound effect on him as an impressionable teenager when he joined up to when he left as a seasoned campaigner at the ripe old age of 19!

Within two years of returning home he was married. Although we do not know very much about his first wife, we do know that she had a profound effect on him, not just in terms of love and marriage and bearing their children, but also in terms of forming and framing his moral, religious and ethical views that were later to be represented in his preaching and writings.

His wife was a devoted, genuine and pious woman and she bought two books to the marriage (books being a relatively rare and important item in those days for ordinary families such as the Bunyans), and these books were called Plain Man's Pathway to Heaven and Practice of Piety.

It is to be wondered whether Bunyan might have suffered from what we might call today *post-traumatic stress disorder,* coming out of 3 years of war fighting against the King. And whilst we don't know this for certain, no doubt he was changed by the experience and was both searching for meaning and open to new ways of thinking and believing. For whilst the old order was being challenged and usurped no one really knew what the new order was or should be.

Bunyan claims that one day he was on the village green and he heard a voice from the heavens and the voice asked him:

"Wilt thou leave thy sins and go to Heaven? Or have thy sins and go to Hell?"

Whilst modern thinking and psychiatry might want to have Bunyan committed for hearing voices on the village green, it is important to suspend judgement and at least accept that for him, something deeply profound and life changing happened to him. For him it was as real as the grass he was standing on, and yet he didn't know exactly what this meant and what the ramifications were to be for him personally.

All he knew for sure was that it meant one thing and one thing alone and that was change. But what to change and how to change?

Shortly afterwards he met some women who were founder members of the Bedford Free Church and this too had a deep effect on him. So much so that he joined their church as a member. Shortly afterwards he also joined a Nonconformist group in the area being run by an ex Royalist officer (bearing in mind that Bunyan had fought on the Parliamentary side). In time Bunyan himself began preaching this new "faith" and also began writing about his beliefs.

It seems that whilst today we have a general view that the time of Cromwell was one of Puritan strictness it seems that there was in fact a good degree of religious tolerance and new ideas and new beliefs were allowed, so long as they didn't challenge the authority of the Commonwealth and the Protector.

The 1650's were a very important time for Bunyan as he tried to find his post conflict self and role and establish a family with his wife. However, he then lost her at a relatively young age and then had to bring up their four young children himself. He then subsequently married someone quite a bit younger than himself and began to establish himself as a preacher and minister and also published his first book: *Gospel Truths Opened.*

With his new wife and children fairly settled, the way seemed to be open for Bunyan to champion his beliefs in relative freedom.

In 1660 the country rejected the experiment of living without a monarchy and Charles II was invited back from France and offered the throne that had been taken away from his father. Whilst much modern perception holds that Charles II brought freedom, gaiety and levity back to what had been a grey, puritanical and intolerant existence, in many ways the opposite was true, especially in matters of religious belief and teaching.

So much so that Bunyan was arrested for his religious beliefs and preaching under the Conventicle Act of 1593 which made it illegal to attend a religious gathering outside a church with more than five people other than members of one's family. This Act has never been repealed so be warned!

Bunyan was charged with having:

"devilishly and perniciousy abstained from coming to church to hear divine service" and having held *"several unlawful meetings and conventicles, to the great disturbance and distraction of the good subjects of this kingdom".*

The maximum sentence for such an offence was supposed to be 3 months in prison, but because Bunyan refused to recant his beliefs he ended up spending no less than 12 years in prison for what was meant to be a 3 month offence! This caused great hardship to his family but he refused to be bowed or broken or compromise his principles.

Bunyan In Bedford Gaol.

It was whilst he was in Bedford Gaol that he began writing his seminal and most famous work – The Pilgrim's Progress, although it wasn't finally published until 1678 which was some years after Bunyan was finally released from gaol.

It is clearly part, if not fully autobiographical in its content and is an incredible work on many levels, standing on its merits as a work of literary genius to being a treatise on religion, politics, society, philosophy, morality and ethics and much more.

One doesn't have to agree with Bunyan's views to find merit in his works. It sets the template for so many works that followed in the future where the chief protagonist or hero goes on a journey to find themselves, redemption and the truth or all three. The influence of Bunyan can be seen on a vast number of writers from then on including Tolkien in Lord of the Rings with Frodo's journey being based on that of Christian in The Pilgrim's Progress.

Curiously enough, the 20th century marks a strong revival in the power and influence of Bunyan's work on creative and philosophical thinking. The acclaimed English composer Ralph Vaughan Williams put it in opera form and it was first performed by the English National Opera in 1951.

Tolkien's Lord of the Rings was first published in 1954, and whilst it is not known whether he saw the opera it is hard to believe that being such a well-educated man that he didn't know about it and was therefore probably inspired by it in writing his own story of Middle Earth and Frodo's own journey.

Certainly there are parallels to be seen within the two journeys, and also many other literary ones that follow Bunyan's legacy with as many variations on the theme as writers that followed it.

Bunyan himself certainly doesn't spare those who disagree with his religious views in the book, for most characters who are of a different persuasion to him tend to end up in hell rather than the Celestial City (heaven) to which his hero Christian aspires.

Whilst Bunyan has his own filters and biases it is clear that his works weren't fashioned out of thin air or any other kind of air for that matter. They were fashioned at the coal face of life and inside the mine of his search for truth.

Is The Pilgrim's Progress a work of fact or fiction?

That is a fascinating question, and really the answer doesn't lie so much inside the book but much more inside the reader and what they bring to the book rather than what the book brings to them.

A cynic certainly won't get much out of it, in the same way that no one ever gets much change or merit out of a cynic.

Whatever one thinks of Christian and his journey within The Pilgrim's Progress we can all identify and empathise with the fact of being on a journey and a search for truth and possibly seeking some kind of redemption or even salvation.

Along the way we all meet many trials and tribulations and lots of other people who sometimes help us and other times don't. And sometimes we ourselves are these other people that other people meet!

At other times when we read the book the "other person" we meet on the journey is in fact ourselves, but a different self to the one we were before starting the book. I certainly know that for myself this was true when I read the book for the first time when I was 15 years old. At the time of teenage change and confusion and searching for identity inside a world badly lost, or so it seemed to me, I found a new part of myself that I didn't even know was there.

And whilst I became somewhat clearer as to who and what I wasn't and wasn't going to be, the answer as to who and what I was and what I could and would be wasn't at all clear. But then perhaps that is the way it is always supposed to be? For a vision needs time for the mist and fog to clear before it can appear.

In the hands of some lesser writers the quotation from Bunyan might seem somewhat trite, clever or witty.

Clearly these words come from a man who knew what it was like to live life from the heart and with a heart. They are not the words of an academic, but come from the heart of a man who knew what hardship was like, who knew privation and pain and suffering, who knew what it was like to take a stand on a matter of principle when it would have been far easier to conform and take the line of least resistance. And yet he didn't.

Christian in Pilgrim's Progress didn't take the line of least resistance either, although he tries to a few times. Thank goodness he did because if he didn't then there wouldn't have been much of a book!

One of my favourite passages of the book is the part where Christian wanders off away from his friend and companion and meets someone called Talkative who espouses all sorts of truths and wisdoms to him. I remember reading these truths and wisdoms for the first time and thinking that they were profound, deep and truly amazing.

Yet when Christian meets up again with Faithful and effusively wants to tell Faithful all about his wonderful new friend called Talkative. Faithful immediately knows that something is wrong and that Christian has not deepened in his journey towards truth but wandered away from it and become tainted and distracted by the empty words that Talkative preaches but doesn't live.

When Talkative is challenged by Faithful, despite Christian's urgings not to do so, Talkative is indeed found to be wanting in the substance department of the matters he speaks of and thus is something of a hypocrite. In today's language he doesn't walk the walk but merely talks the talk.

I can still remember the feeling of having been taken in hook, line and sinker by Talkative. (How did I not realise what was coming next with a name like Talkative!) Still what can one expect from a very naïve and gullible 15 year old?

But I then thought, if I wasn't going to be what the priests who taught me thought I should be, then what was I going to actually be in the place of that? Plus, all the other parties involved in my "education" as well including parents, society, friends and of course the biggest conspirator of all in keeping me from the truth of myself, me!

If I wasn't going to be what everyone else wanted me to be, then what was I going to be and how on earth would I begin the journey of finding out who and what I really was and what was it that I was supposed to be and become?

I wasn't found when I read The Pilgrim's Progress for the first time. Quite the opposite in fact, for I think I realised that I was in fact lost, that I didn't know who or what I was.

But having been rumbled like Talkative was by Faithful I felt something inside that resonated about the quote from Bunyan about the importance of what lives inside a person's heart as being far more important that what does or doesn't come out of their mouth.

In particular, when Faithful challenges Talkative with these words:

"Doth your life and conversation testify the same? Or standeth your religion in word or tongue, and not in deed and truth?"

Talkative is not used to being challenged about the substance behind his fine words and soon withdraws because the scrutiny reveals that he is in fact a hypocrite. His deception cannot stand the light of truth being shone on his life to show what he is really like.

Somehow the saying of Bunyan reminds one of the maxim that it is better to keep one's mouth shut and let the world think that one is a fool rather than open it and remove all doubt whatsoever!

There is also the saying that talk is cheap and in the absence of feeling and resonance with a living and lived truth it most certainly is.

It costs nothing to fashion fine words.

It certainly didn't cost John Bunyan nothing for him to come to the wisdom that it is far better to have a heart without words than words without a heart.

For that fact alone the world has a lot to be grateful to John Bunyan for. In helping each one of us to locate our own inner pilgrim and maybe find our own way home to the truth of who and what we really are, and maybe, just maybe, that is enough for us all to succeed in being successful human beings?

A loving heart is the beginning of all knowledge.

Thomas Carlyle

Thomas Carlyle was a Scottish philosopher, mathematician, historian and social commentator who lived in the 19th century. In some ways he was both a pioneer and a reflection of some of the times that he lived in for he was serious, somewhat dour and concerned with matters of social importance and moral duty.

He appears not to have been the most light-hearted or humorous man who ever lived and in many ways seems to fit the stereotype of the Scottish austere, serious, granite faced and granite living, worrying about destiny and damnation, Puritan.

Here is a photo of him possibly to add weight to that view.

Clearly not the happiest man in the world by the look of him!

Still first impressions can be deceiving, for anyone who branded Economics as being *"That dismal science"* can't be all bad or lacking a sense of humour!

In today's language if someone says that they are an economist then perhaps an equivalent response might be: *"Get a life son!"*

Carlyle was in fact a very influential thinker in his time, and moved in very wide and diverse circles of philosophical and social thought and was for example a close friend of Ralph Waldo Emerson. It is said that his 1837 book *The French Revolution: A History,* was the inspiration for Charles Dickens' book *A Tale of Two Cities* which was published in 1859.

Carlyle was a much more complex and complicated man than any simple stereotype could define for he was in many ways unique. His life span saw the rise and all-pervading influence of the Industrial Revolution and its largely materialistic, post Enlightenment, reductionist view of life take hold of many Western societies. He also sought to find within human existence balancing philosophical, moral and spiritual premises that would help people find context and meaning for their lives and how to do good.

His prolific mathematical skills made him an excellent analyst and rationalist who was happy to deal in logic and reason in the search for truth. But he also had a fascination with romanticism, transcendentalism and religion as being important ingredients within finding out who we are and what our responsibilities as human beings are too.

More of Thomas Carlyle at the end of this chapter.

Meanwhile, his quotation asks a very important question before we even get into the detail about its meaning and application and that is:

Just what is it that we think knowledge is?

For without looking at that question we can easily begin with a series of assumptions that we all agree we know what knowledge is, or that there is perhaps only one kind of knowledge. In fact, there may be many kinds and levels to knowledge and indeed situations where different "knowledges" disagree or clash. Is knowledge the same thing as truth? It would seem not to be, as for starters it is a completely different word!

There is much to consider and be aware of for even in framing the question – what do we think knowledge is, we are asking ourselves to think about it as opposed to what we feel about it.

Thinking is something that is done in the head, at least most scientists think that is where we think, though some are now not quite so sure with alternative theories of things like morphic fields and the Zero Point Field offering different views of such processes as thinking.

Putting that debate aside for a moment, it is easy to see that in the modern world that knowledge is seen to be something that is mostly acquired through functions that go on in the brain; things like thinking, analysis, deduction, reasoning, comparison, logic, calculation, referencing, remembering, accepting and rejecting, theorising, systemising and the like.

In short, thinking is linking.

Yet whilst thinking is a profound source of connection to reality that we know it clearly isn't the only source of knowledge we have, because we have more than one feedback system available to us to give us input, feelings, senses, awareness, emotions and lots more.

For example, we know when we feel that we are in love or that we care passionately about something for it fills up every fibre of our being. Yet it is clearly not something that comes from logic or reasoning alone or at all.

If thinking knowledge comes from a bottom up process, then things like love come from a transcendent or top down process. We usually fall in love and then find out afterwards the reason why! Then when we start to think about the reasons or overthink them that is when things often start to go wrong. We lose or disconnect from that original feeling, and then the brain tries to get in the way and hog all the action and take control of both the knowledge and the relationship.

In approaching this quotation from Thomas Carlyle then, it is useful to explore what knowledge might mean unto itself.

The dictionary says that knowledge is based upon experience and consciousness. These are two essential aspects of something being real and tangible rather than merely intellectual and theoretical.

Until one has tasted asparagus one has absolutely no knowledge whatsoever of what they taste like. Until one has listened to Mozart one has no idea whatsoever of what the music is like or more particularly what it causes when one listens to it. If one has never been to the seaside, then there can be no real knowledge of what it is like or what it feels like to paddle or swim in the sea.

Until one has fallen in love one has absolutely no idea of what it is actually like to be overtaken to the degree that one is almost consumed by these feelings.

The theory of something, or indeed everything, is never the same as the feeling of one thing.

Until a person has tasted garlic, beetroot, aniseed or whisky they will never know whether or not they like them.

You might get a reasonable idea of what someone or something is like from what other people tell you about them or it, but until you actually experience meeting them or it you won't know for sure.

I well remember my father trying to have a difficult conversation with his rather difficult, taciturn, fourteen year old son (me!) about the facts of life. (A bit late in the day Dad to be approaching such a subject, but I put it down to Catholic shame and guilt about the subject!)

Anyway, he tried to approach the subject as carefully as he could and produced a little booklet that was going to explain to me all the turgid stuff I needed to know about the secret and not to be discussed world of sex.

And me in my *"I know everything because I am a teenager"* mode told him in no uncertain terms that I didn't need his explanation nor the tacky pamphlet because there was nothing in there or that he could tell me that I didn't already know!

Of course there was nothing I didn't know already about the subject matter. The only slight problem I had with my vast knowledge of the subject matter was that since the age of nine I had been to boys only schools and taught in turn by nuns and then priests. I therefore had absolutely no experience of even meeting girls yet alone finding out what made them tick. Nor whether any of them could or would like me, yet alone maybe hold my hand whilst I read the pamphlet Dad had given me and tried to work out how to get to what was on the last page!

When I finally did get to meet these strange creatures called girls a couple of years later, all my "knowledge" faded into oblivion as I quickly adopted my winning ways with them by becoming a gibbering and incoherent wreck in front of them.

The first piece of "knowledge" I acquired from the first one I tried to get acquainted with was when I asked her what she thought she wanted to do when she left school and she said that she thought she might become a nun!

Was it me that inspired that thought in her I wondered?

As my knowledge about girls and affairs of the heart dissipated into whatever comes before rock bottom so did my confidence and hopes that I would ever get to apply the knowledge in Dad's manual.

I wonder what happened to Loretta?
Did her mother ever give her the girl's equivalent pamphlet that my Dad gave me?
Maybe she joined one of those silent orders of nuns who shut themselves away from the world of men and pray a lot?

I hope she is happy whatever the case.

No wonder Shakespeare said: *"A little knowledge is a dangerous thing."*

However, no knowledge at all is even more dangerous and no knowledge but thinking one has lots of knowledge and expertise has to be the worst of the lot.

For no knowledge implies that a person has neither experience nor consciousness.

But what actually is consciousness?

We say that when someone is in a coma or has been knocked out by a blow to the head that they are unconscious. They are neither awake nor aware of who they are or where they are. It is not the same as being as being asleep for that is a natural state that we all go through each and every day.

Being unconscious therefore is not a normal state to find oneself in because in that state one is not awake, alert or aware.

This suggests that perhaps there are different states or levels of consciousness beyond the physical level of not being unconscious, if that's not using a double negative which it is!

It seems reasonably clear and obvious that there are indeed different levels of consciousness or awareness because a baby has limited awareness of who and what it is other than its immediate surroundings and need of things like warmth, food and sleep. In fact, a baby doesn't recognise itself in the mirror until enough development takes place in the brain to enable the child to have sufficient self-awareness and recognition of who and what one is as a separate and unique being from everyone else.

Therefore, the first level of consciousness is the awareness of self as an individual in one's own right at physical level. Nearly everyone manages to reach this level of consciousness without too much problem, and yet the same principle of consciousness applies at more advanced levels too.

As we get older and our various human systems develop and grow both physically and emotionally we start to form things like identity and personality, based on a whole variety of things such as genetics, society, family, beliefs, religion and education.

These influences all affect our consciousness of who and what we think we are and what we think we can and should be and do.

Our experiences shape our consciousness and our consciousness determines our goals, aspirations, hopes, fears, beliefs and actions.

The difficulty or challenge in this is trying to discover or reveal whether consciousness is strictly a physical thing or whether there are aspects to it that relate to non-physical or less physical aspects. Are there aspects of our experience that genuinely live in the realms of what might be called ecstasy, religious feelings, revelation, spirituality and more?

In other words, do we have systems within us that we may not even be conscious of that can access certain truths about our existence that the systems that we are conscious of – such as the nerves, lungs, spleen, immune system and so on can't?

Could the heart itself be an important part of that system?

Whether that is true or not cannot be proven using a lower system of machine measurement, but certainly most cultures seem to have a belief, awareness and consciousness that the heart does have an important part to play in activating the higher aspects of our consciousness.

The nervous system clearly has a vital role play as an information and feedback system and what is happening to us moment by moment as life happens upon us. But is there a higher information service that can connect us into a higher form of consciousness?

Is this the state of enlightenment that the Buddha spoke of for example?

Or the collective unconscious as spoken of by Carl Jung as another example?

Is this the gate that Carlyle was seeking in his quotation?

It seems however that Carlyle didn't necessarily embody all of the happiness of the heart that the head may only dream of.

His marriage to Jane Welsh, who was an important literary figure in her own right, was at times strained and difficult. Indeed, one of Carlyle's biographers even claimed that the marriage was never in fact consummated.

Samuel Butler wrote this rather unkind commentary on the Carlyle's marriage:

It was very good of God to let Carlyle and Mrs Carlyle marry one another, and so make only two people miserable and not four.

Although their relationship may appear to have been stretched and strained, sometimes to the limit, perhaps the truth is that it was simply more honest and more equal than most. For in amongst the difficulties there was also a great mutual respect and affection for the couple wrote each other over 9000 letters during the course of their shared lifetime together. People don't write each other 9000 letters if they don't have some shared values and feelings.

After his wife passed away suddenly in 1866 Carlyle was deeply affected by this event and he posthumously had published Reminiscences of Jane Welsh Carlyle which was kind to her memory and deeply critical of himself.

Carlyle had a brilliant mind of that there is no doubt.

But he also had a knowing that the head needed to yield to the heart in the matters of deepest truth. Being moved was more important than rational argument alone.

He knew the pain of being with and without those feelings and he also knew that he himself wasn't the perfect embodiment of what he yearned for, longed for.

We may all have our imperfections, but that does not prevent or bar any of us feeling, being moved by and responding to the power of those things that help perfect our experience of the most high and deep feelings that exist and carry the hopes of ourselves and perhaps the very Universe itself.

My heart has followed all my days, something I cannot name.

Don Marquis

Today we live in a world where pretty much everything has a name, including you. For although your first experience of life outside the womb wasn't really focused on what your name was, but rather on getting a first gulp of air into your lungs, pretty soon the world began to make decisions about who and what you were and also who and what you might be and become.

If your parents were married, then it was also pretty certain as to what surname you would inherit and even if they were not married the choices were fairly limited as to what credible options you would have. Your surname would further define which family you belonged to and what that might mean for you in terms of extended family, tribe, class, religion and so on.

Welcome to the world of where you fit in!

Then a possibly harder task began for our parents because they had to consider what your first name or as we often call it in the West, your Christian name, might be. Some parents even have the name of their baby decided before the baby is actually born, and the reasons for choosing a first name for the baby are about as many and varied as the number of babies born.

It could be that a certain name is going through a popularity boom, or perhaps you are named after some transient celebrity who is famous today and gone tomorrow, or even after some relative, or worse still you are given the same name as your parent which says a lot about whose footsteps you are expected to follow in. Good luck with overcoming that one!

We have names for this and names for that to such a degree that most of the words in the dictionary are in fact the names for and of things.

Even our first words are expected to be names with the hope the first intelligible utterances we make are hopefully going to be either Momma or Dadda or similar.

So we move from the world where nothing has a name but everything is felt and experienced, to one where everything is named and very little is experienced without somehow a name, a title, a label, a condition, a syndrome, an explanation being put upon it. This is done so that we can then safely place things in the known world where all unknown things need to be placed so they can do no harm to the self-view of who and what we and others think we are.

But the who and what you are comes from the place that is way above and beyond the place that names come from.

For if you had never heard of or seen an elephant and then suddenly came across one out of the blue it's hardly likely that you would simply go: *"Oh look it's an elephant."*

You would be completely overtaken by the enormity of the experience, and you would have absolutely no idea what to call this unique encounter with the world's largest land animal. All your systems would be heightened and on total alert within this awe inspiring moment.

You would absolutely no idea whatsoever as to what you should call this creature in front of you and nor would you know how to react to it, though no doubt caution would feature fairly high on the list due to the sheer size of the animal before you.

How would you convey your experience to your friends and family when you return home and try and tell them of your encounter with something they too have no reference fields for either?

So why can't all of our lives be in this heightened state of alertness and awareness all or more of the time?

Somehow we manage to find ways of making the extraordinary ordinary and indeed manageable and a key factor in this is naming them.

But what if we managed to find the way to return the awe and wonder of what things truly are in their essence and being lives by somehow un-naming them?

This is where a wondrous poem by Don Marquis that contains the above quotation can most certain help.

And here it is in full.

The Name

IT shifts and shifts from form to form,
It drifts and darkles, gleams and glows;
It is the passion of the storm,
The poignance of the rose;
Through changing shapes, through devious
ways,
By noon or night, through cloud or flame,

My heart has followed all my days
Something I cannot name.

In sunlight on some woman's hair,
Or starlight in some woman's eyne,
Or in low laughter smothered where
Her red lips wedded mine,
My heart hath known, and thrilled to know,
This unnamed presence that it sought;
And when my heart hath found it so,
"Love is the name," I thought.

Sometimes when sudden afterglows
In futile glory storm the skies
Within their transient gold and rose
The secret stirs and dies;
Or when the trampling morn walks o'er
The troubled seas, with feet of flame,
My awed heart whispers, "Ask no more,
For Beauty is the name!"

Or dreaming in old chapels where
The dim aisles pulse with murmurings
That part are music, part are prayer--
(Or rush of hidden wings)
Sometimes I lift a startled head
To some saint's carven countenance,
Half fancying that the lips have said,
All names mean God, perchance!"

Truly a poem of great and moving beauty. Yet it also contains an ache within it and a longing for these feelings, these moments, this resonance, this state of being, this art, to be embodied within the noblest art of all which is also called living.

Living in witness and withness as was meant to be and can still be and always be.

If one must give a name to this place from which all this essence of beingness emanates it can only be The Source.

The way we remember and find our way back to this sacred place is with the heart as our guide, mentor, friend and counsellor.

Imagine a place where names no longer are labels, but come to mean – God, perchance.

Not the God that hides in formal places of form and conformity. But the God that says: "I have no name and I am that I am."

Everything returns to the source of its arising just as everything arises from that source in the first place.

But perhaps with VAT added.

VAT to mean Value Added Truth.

Afterword

Everything in the Universe moves, even dead stuff!
However why move in the way and style of dead stuff
when you can be – alive!

Even things that we think aren't alive still move, because
everything is made up of atoms and particles and they all
vibrate. And everything that vibrates creates waves and
ripples that radiate out from the source and affect
everything they come into contact with, either directly or
indirectly.

This includes everything we think and feel.

Therefore, everything we think and feel really matters.

This is a two-way street however, for not only do we
affect everything else but everything else also affects us.
In fact, who and what you are is largely a matter of what
you have allowed yourself to be influenced and affected
by, both for good and for bad.

This is a very empowering proposition to consider,
because it says we can make more decisions about what
we will and won't be influenced by and why.

So what would you wish to be influenced by and why?

Consider for a moment what you are in fact made up of.
Yes, there are bones, blood, nerves and cells etc. but
beyond that you are made up of sunlight from a source
way, way back in the life and origins of the Universe
itself. And that my friend is a very cool thought indeed!

Therefore, in order to be the best you that you can
possibly be, wouldn't it make sense to let in more of this

life giving and life affirming force as much and as often as you can?

Well you can, no problem at all.

All you have to do is – open up your heart and let the sunshine in!

And then out. ☺

About the Author

Tony Kearney was born in New Zealand where he grew up and studied at University. Having qualified as a lawyer he then embarked on travels around the world before settling in London where he practised as a lawyer for nearly 25 years.

He has travelled widely taking workshops, seminars and giving lectures on many diverse subjects from matters of personal, planetary and global change, to children's education, to gender relations and many other related topics.

In 2006 he moved to Ireland where he now lives and furthers his work in these areas whilst also working as an eclectic mix of writer, consultant, trainer, facilitator, farmer and mediator.

Contact: You can find out more about Tony and what he does together with details of how to get in touch with him at:

www.tonykearney.com

Lightning Source UK Ltd.
Milton Keynes UK
UKHW020814300921
391439UK00013B/850